M. Jones

The Story of Captain Cook's Three Voyages Round the World

Fifth Edition

M. Jones

The Story of Captain Cook's Three Voyages Round the World
Fifth Edition

ISBN/EAN: 9783744788298

Printed in Europe, USA, Canada, Australia, Japan

Cover: Foto ©ninafisch / pixelio.de

More available books at **www.hansebooks.com**

COOK LANDING AT MALLICOLLI, NEW H. BRIDES.

THE STORY
OF
CAPTAIN COOK'S
THREE VOYAGES
ROUND THE WORLD.

TOLD BY M. JONES,

AUTHOR OF "STORIES OF THE OLDEN TIME," ETC.

FIFTH EDITION.

CASSELL PETTER & GALPIN:
LONDON, PARIS & NEW YORK.

PREFACE.

THE narrative of Captain Cook's discoveries is one full of interest, not only as revealing what at that time were new lands and new people, but as showing with transparent clearness the character of him who accomplished the great work which it records. It is, however, very long; and its length is in part made up of matter not very attractive, either to the general reader or to young folks. I have, therefore, for the latter more especially, prepared from it this simple story of what the great Captain saw and did in his Three Voyages Round the World.

M. J.

CONTENTS.

CHAP. I.—FIRST VOYAGE.—From England to Tahiti—
Life in the Island 1
CHAP. II.—Tahiti, and its People 13
CHAP. III.—Huaheine, Ulietea, and other of the Society
Islands—New Zealand . . . 24
CHAP. IV.—Explorations of New Zealand—Its People . 33
CHAP. V.—New South Wales—Narrow Escape from
Wreck—Natives 49
CHAP. VI.—New Guinea—Savu—Batavia—The Cape—
Home 67
CHAP. VII.—SECOND VOYAGE.—Objects of the Voyage
—In the Ice—Cross the Antarctic Circle—Lose
sight of the "Adventure" 81
CHAP. VIII.—New Zealand, Queen Charlotte's Sound—
The Society Islands again 96
CHAP. IX.—Friendly Islands—New Zealand again—Sail
to the South—Turned back by Ice—Easter Island
—The Marquesas—Society Islands—A Review of
War Canoes 110
CHAP. X.—New Hebrides—New Caledonia—Leave the
South Pacific Ocean 129
CHAP. XI.—Christmas Sound, Tierra del Fuego—Sea
Lions—Discoveries in the South Atlantic—Again
turned back by Ice—Murder of Furneaux's Boat's
Crew—Home 145

CONTENTS.

CHAP. XII.—THIRD VOYAGE.—Search for a Short Passage between the North Pacific and the North Atlantic—Van Diemen's Land—Third Visit to New Zealand—Islands Discovered and Revisited—Games and Entertainments—King of the Friendly Islands 155

CHAP. XIII.—Omai at Tahiti—Human Sacrifices in the Society Islands—Cockroaches—Dealings with the Natives 178

CHAP. XIV.—Discovery of the Sandwich Islands—Northwest Coast of North America—Natives . . 188

CHAP. XV.—Anchor on the Coast of Asia—Natives—Arctic Ice—Sea Horses—Russian Traders—Sandwich Islands—Owhyhee (Hawaii) Discovered . 207

CHAP. XVI.—Ceremonies at the Morai—The Taboo—State Visit of the King—Funeral of a Sailor—Leave the Island, but compelled to Return . . 221

CHAP. XVII.—Karakakooa Bay—Natives Troublesome—Attack on the English—Captain Cook Slain . 232

CHAP. XVIII.—Leave Karakakooa Bay—Harbour of St. Peter and St. Paul—Russian Hospitality—Dog Sledges—The Capital of Kamschatka—Generous Kindness of the Russian Governor—Try again for the North West Passage, and again Foiled—Walrus and White Bears—Death of Captain Clerke—Return to St. Peter and St. Paul—China—Home . 243

ILLUSTRATIONS.

	PAGE
COOK LANDING AT MALLICOLLO, NEW HEBRIDES	Frontispiece.
VIEW OF CAPE HORN	4
VIEW IN TAHITI	9
VIEW OF TAHITI	13
ARMS AND INSTRUMENTS, SOCIETY ISLANDS	21
HOUSE OF WORSHIP, HUAHEINE	25
PATOO-PATOOS	35
NEW ZEALAND PAH	39
INTERIOR OF PAH	41
NEW ZEALAND FLAX	47
AUSTRALIAN NATIVES AND HUT	51
PORT JACKSON	54
KANGAROOS	60
NATIVES OF NEW SOUTH WALES	62
NATIVES OF NEW GUINEA	68
BOOBIES	77
TABLE MOUNTAIN, CAPE OF GOOD HOPE	84
MAN AND WOMAN OF NEW ZEALAND	91
WATER SPOUT	94
MATAVAI BAY, TAHITI	100
BAY OF HUAHEINE, SOCIETY ISLANDS	103
STATUES, EASTER ISLAND	119
TATTOOED MARQUESAN	121
DOUBLE CANOE, SOCIETY ISLANDS	123

ILLUSTRATIONS.

	PAGE
View in the Isle of Tanna	136
Man and Woman of Tanna	138
View in New Caledonia	139
Man and Woman of New Caledonia	141
Double Canoe, New Caledonia	142
Native of Tierra del Fuego	145
Fuegian Wigwams	146
Ice off Cape Horn	148
Seals	158
Tahiti	178
Otoo, King of Tahiti	180
Valley in the Island of Huaheine	185
Canadian Pine	197
Karakakooa Bay, Owhyhee (Hawaii)	219
Polar Bear	256
Albatross	258

THE STORY OF CAPTAIN COOK.

CHAPTER I.

FIRST VOYAGE ROUND THE WORLD, IN 1768, 1769, 1770, AND 1771.—FROM ENGLAND TO TAHITI.—LIFE IN THE ISLAND.

IN the year 1768, it was determined by the English Government to send an expedition into the Southern Seas, not only for the purpose of making an important astronomical observation, but for that of exploring those waters, which were little known at the time.

The commander of this expedition was one of England's great men—good, as well as great. He was of humble birth. He first learned his letters from an old woman who kept the little village school of Marton, in Yorkshire, where he was born in 1728. Whilst a mere child he was apprenticed to a shopkeeper, not far from Whitby. But shop-keeping he did not like, so was not long in getting rid of all ties to the counter and yardstick: giving himself up instead to the hard life of a common sailor on board a collier. It was a hard life; but it was a good school for him: the navigation of that part of the British seas that lies between the north and south of England being reckoned intricate and hazardous. And in this humble service, James Cook, the future circumnavigator of the globe—for it is he of whom we are writing—acquitted himself so well as to rise to the rank of mate. At the age of twenty-seven, when war with France was hot, and good seamen much needed, he found himself in no little danger of being "pressed," as the phrase then was; that is, of being seized by Government, and compelled to serve in the Navy, whether he liked it or not. He took a perfectly novel way of avoiding the risk—he went and offered himself as a volunteer; and this wise step was the making of the man. His skill, his untiring industry, his genius and good conduct, rapidly raised him from his first rating as "able seaman" to that of lieutenant in the Royal Navy, an appointment to which he was gazetted May 25th, 1768, and for the express purpose of commanding the projected expedition. The delicate astronomical observation, which was also an object of the undertaking, was that of the passing of the planet Venus over the sun's face; and Otaheite, or, as it is now called, Tahiti, one of the Society Islands, was the spot fixed upon for the purpose. This island was discovered by a Spaniard in 1606, and had been visited by the English under Captain Wallis, a short time before Cook's going thither.

The ship commanded by Cook on this occasion was named the "Endeavour." She had been originally built for the coal trade, and was of only 370 tons burden—a small vessel for such great work; but it is said only bad workmen quarrel with their tools. . She had ten swivel and ten carriage guns—the former, as their name imports, being so mounted as to enable them to be pointed in any required direction; together with ammunition, and stores of various kinds, to trade with the natives in those distant seas, as well as to supply the wants of those on board. The ship was victualled for eighteen months, and had a crew of eighty-five persons, including the commander, Mr. Banks (afterwards Sir Joseph), Dr. Solander, and Mr. Green: these latter gentlemen being concerned only in the scientific part of the expedition.

Cook hoisted his pennant on board on the 25th of May; but it was not until the 26th of August that the "Endeavour" sailed from Plymouth, right into a hard gale, which, heralded—as sailors suppose—by birds called Mother Cary's chickens, knocked her about to good purpose before she was far from English shores. The rich and beautiful island of Madeira was first touched at, affording them water, and good fresh provisions, at rather a high price. Next came Rio, where Cook was not very civilly treated by the ignorant viceroy; then a landing on the wretched coast of Tierra del Fuego, where Banks and Solander, out botanising nearly lost their lives from the cold. Five minutes' sleep there so shrunk the muscles of Dr. Solander's feet, that when he awoke his shoes fell off; and two of their black servants, who had also given way to the stupefying influence of extreme cold, could not be aroused at all. The poor creatures were obliged to be left to their fate, with branches of trees spread under and heaped above them, in the forlorn hope of imparting a little warmth to their bodies. And this was summer in that part of the world. Finally, after doubling, or sailing round, the long-dreaded Cape Horn, which, like many other things much feared, did not turn out half as bad as was expected, the "Endeavour" reached her destination, in the lovely island of Tahiti, on the 13th of April, 1769. Many beautiful little specks of land, amid the wide waste of ocean waters, had been discovered during the run from Cape Horn to Tahiti, and to these names were given by Cook. In approaching the island, numerous canoes were seen paddling to meet them, bringing young plantains and branches of trees, which some of the natives caused our people to understand were signs of friendship. They were accordingly received, and placed about in the rigging of the vessel, to the evident pleasure of those who had brought them.

No sooner had the ship cast anchor in Port Royal Bay—called by the natives Matavai Bay—than she was surrounded by canoes, laden with fruits and various kinds of small fish, which their owners were eager to exchange for beads and other trinkets. They had with them a pig; but the prudent commander knew better than to buy that at the price demanded—a hatchet—seeing that at that rate all the hatchets he possessed would never have bought pork enough for his ship's company; and it could not be expected that the poor creatures would afterwards lower their terms to suit his convenience. So pig had to wait until the owners were content with something less costly than hatchet in exchange.

As the stay of the expedition upon this—at that time—

CAPE HORN.

wild spot, with half-naked and entirely uncivilised savages around them, was likely to be prolonged, great precautions were needed to prevent dissensions, which might end in bloodshed, arising between the English crew and their native visitors. Cook's sagacity and goodness were quite equal to this; he laid it down as a law in his small domain—the little 370-ton brig, with its living cargo of less than eighty souls, under his command—that all humanity and kindliness should be shown towards the scrambling horde of savages by which they were surrounded; that trafficking for provisions between the ship's crew and the islanders should be managed solely by one person, appointed by himself; and that the usual strict, wholesome naval discipline should extend to this out-of-the-way corner of the earth.

As soon as the "Endeavour" was fairly secured in her moorings, a party, under the commander, went ashore, and were received by hundreds of awe-stricken natives, carrying their symbols of peace and good will—green branches of trees. The first of these who ventured near the strangers, crawling almost on all fours, handed his branch to them, who, to show equal kindliness, after accepting it, gathered boughs for themselves, and, each man bearing one, accompanied their new friends to a spot where the natives first threw their branches on the ground, and then desired the English to do the same with theirs. A little procession of marines and gentlemen was accordingly formed, and, marching along, each one with great solemnity dropped his branch on those that already strewed the place. Next day another visit was made on shore, when presents were exchanged between our people and the natives; a couple of fowls and some perfumed native cloth were given to the captain and Mr. Banks, the chief Tootahah getting in return a laced cravat and pocket kerchief, with which he seemed highly delighted. All were exceedingly friendly; food was offered to the English, and they made a very tolerable dinner on fish, bread-fruit, cocoa-nuts, and plantains, dressed in the country fashion—their hosts eating some of their fish raw. Whilst they were enjoying themselves in this amicable manner, however, two of the gentlemen suddenly announced that their pockets had been picked; and Mr. Banks, by way of giving emphasis to the complaint, struck the butt-end of his musket smartly on the ground. Instantly all was uproar: the house was cleared in a trice, not more than the chief and four or five others venturing to remain after this, presumed, warlike demonstration.

In this difficulty the chief, Toubourai Tamaide, with whom they had previously made friends, behaved like an honest man and a gentleman. Leading Mr. Banks by the hand to a large quantity of native cloth that lay there, he made signs that he was welcome to any or all of it as compensation for the loss; and when this was rejected—the restitution of the stolen articles being alone required—he hastened away, returning presently with a portion of them, nor did he rest until the whole had been restored to the owners.

This good fellow was on another occasion himself suspected—unjustly, as it turned out—of thieving; and the expression of his strong, honest indignation at the shabby charge was worthy of a civilised good Christian—passionately intimating by signs that he would be willing to have his throat cut, if he were ever guilty of such a thing. It cost Mr. Banks some petting and soothing before he had smoothed down the justly-ruffled feelings of his indignant acquaintance.

The precautions taken against offending their outlandish friends were most thoughtful and excellent, and at first appeared successful; but, alas! head and hands do not always agree. The cautious and admirable commander, having made arrangements for taking his astronomical observations, went off with a small party to examine the interior of this new and beautiful country. No sooner was his back turned than mischief began. One of the natives, to whom thieving came by nature—they stole right and left, men, women, and children, chiefs and common people, and, poor wretches, had had no instruction to modify their evil instincts—laid quick hands upon the musket of the sentry at the little camp left behind, and made off with it. The hasty lad, a midshipman, who commanded the guard, had no more sense than to order the marines to fire on the naked savages thronging around; and as this foolish, wicked volley had no apparent effect upon the startled crowd, one of the chiefs was picked out and shot dead.

Cook would never have done that, and he was justly indignant that things could not be kept proper and right if his back were turned for never so short a time. The natives—and no wonder—were slow in becoming friendly again after this, but at last they came to. Peace-offerings of two young trees were brought to the ship by two of the chiefs, and when these had been graciously accepted, they ventured on board with a most welcome gift of baked pig and bread-fruit, in return for which each of them received a hatchet and a nail, and things went on as comfortably as before: the more so that the natives were reassured by the scrupulous honesty of the commander, who would not cut even a stake without their consent, and also paying for it. Indeed, so determined was he that right should be done to these simple specimens of mankind, that he had the butcher of the vessel tied up and soundly flogged for threatening the life of one of the Tahitian women, because she would not make a bargain with him to his mind on some paltry matter. The natives, in their good nature, tried to beg the rascal off, and when they found it was of no use, fairly cried for disappointment; tears, however, were plentiful with them on the slightest occasion, and, as is usual in such cases, "forgot as soon as shed."

With regard to the native tendency to "picking and stealing," it must be owned there was much in excuse of these poor pagans: nails and beads, and such like objects of admiration, not to mention iron hatchets, and, in due time, a quadrant and the ship's anchor, presented to them precisely the same amount of temptation that jewels and untold silver and gold would to a civilised person; and we know that many such—aye, and called Christians to boot —cannot withstand *this* temptation.

It had been determined to erect a small fort on shore, as a protection for those engaged either in the astronomical observations, or in the general examination of this part of the island. A spot was, in the first place, selected for its site, and around this lines were drawn within which no

VIEW IN TAHITI.

natives, save the two friendly chiefs, who appeared to be important personages, were allowed to enter. To the wondering crowd, who looked on whilst these mysterious lines were being drawn, it was intimated that the ground within them was wanted, for a time, as a sleeping place for the strangers; and to this no objection was made.

The islanders themselves willingly assisted in the work of construction, acting as beasts of burden with much cheerfulness. The commencement of this important undertaking was signalised by serving out pork for dinner; and the kindly natives brought them more bread-fruit and cocoanuts than they could possibly eat. Beads were the purchase-money, in which transaction one thinks the vendors must have come off "second best," seeing they only got one bead, the size of a pea, for half-a-dozen cocoa-nuts or bread-fruits. But value is a thing difficult to determine all the world over.

Mr. Banks slept on shore that night, and the next morning the friendly chief with the long name, Toubourai Tamaide, paid him a visit with a bag-and-baggage party, consisting of himself, his wife and children, and the framework and furnishing of a house which he signified his intention to set up near the English quarters. This, of course, was a valuable neighbour; and the friendship was cemented by his clothing Mr. Banks with two native garments, one of red cloth, the other of matting. This done, he breakfasted on pork and bread-fruit, with salt water for seasoning; after which, lying down on Mr. Banks's bed, he got a sound nap. Toubourai liked to imitate English manners, and in due time got to use a knife and fork at meals with great dexterity. How often, in process of learning to deal with such dangerous weapons, he cut his fingers and pricked his mouth, we are not told.

Soon after this, the body of the poor fellow who had been shot by the hasty midshipman was found, wrapped in his mat and white cloth, laid upon a kind of bier, beneath a shed, about fifteen feet long, eleven broad, and high in proportion, close to his house. Near his head were two cocoa-nut shells, used by the people as cups; at his feet, a bunch of green leaves and dry twigs, stuck in the ground. A young plantain tree—emblem of peace—lay near at hand. At one end of the shed hung strings of palm-nuts; outside it, the stem of a plantain, about five feet in height, supported a cocoa-nut shell of water; roasted bread-fruit was placed in a bag hung on one of the posts of the shed. The natives about did not seem much to like the examination of this simple funeral pile. Perhaps they remembered how cruelly he who lay there had been slaughtered by the friends of those now looking upon his lifeless form.

Of the funeral ceremonies of these people, Mr. Banks was afterwards a spectator, nay, an actor in them; for, in order to gratify his scientific curiosity on the subject, he was obliged to take his part in the solemnities. His mourning dress for the occasion—native fashion—was a small bit of cloth around his waist, and a more ample suit of charcoal and water, so liberally applied, that a considerable portion of his person was as black as a sweep. Others were "got up" in the same manner: one of them, a boy, being blacked all over. Then a procession was formed, from which, as it drew near, the natives fled in wild haste. And no wonder, seeing it was one of the functions of the chief mourner to strike at every one who came near him, with a formidable implement, set with sharks' teeth, inflicting very severe wounds. At the end of its circuit, which lasted half-an-hour, the mourners washed off their black, and there was an end of it.

The bones of their dead, after being wasted by wind and weather, in such exposure as that of the slaughtered man, were consigned to mother earth, in places called *Morai*, which were also used for the worship of their gods. Some of these were on a surprisingly large scale, and of workmanship to excite wonder as well as admiration. One is described as being a vast pile of stone and coral, pyramid-shaped, with a base of 267 feet by 87. It was built in steps, each step being a course of coral stone picked up from the bed of the sea, well worked and polished; with a foundation of rock stone, also wrought. The interior of the mass was filled up with boulders, which appeared to have undergone some shaping process. The whole, though there was no mortar to join the blocks, was compact and firm. The figure of a bird, carved in wood, crowned the top of the pyramid, which was ridged like the roof of a house. Near it lay part of a stone carving of a fish. This pile formed only part of the side of a large square, walled and paved with stone. Near to it were several smaller erections, on wooden pillars, which were supposed to be altars, as offerings of provisions to their gods were placed upon them.

This magnificent Morai belonged to Oberea, one of the chief women of the island, whom previous visitors had taken for its queen. Poor Oberea, who showed kindly attentions to our explorers, had, it seems, "come down in the world:" an invasion of her territories by neighbouring savages having despoiled her of her goods, and thereby injured her position in the country as to rank; just as, some centuries ago, there was in England a duke—George Nevill, Duke of Bedford—who was *un*-duked on account of his poverty.

Towards the end of April the fort, at which English and natives had wrought with such good will, was completed, and, for its purpose, was a place of considerable strength. On two sides there was an earthwork, four and a-half feet high, with a ditch at foot, towards the country, ten feet broad and six deep. To the west, an earthwork, four feet high, with strong stakes driven in at top, sufficed, as the tide flowed up to its base. The east, as the weakest point, had, in addition to two rows of water-casks full of water, a couple of four-pounders; whilst six swivel guns were placed so as to oppose all attack from the direction of the woods in that quarter. The ship's guns commanded the whole. Five-and-forty men garrisoned the entrenchments, which were guarded, in regular military fashion, with sentries, formally "relieved" from time to time.

The shore life of the little party would have been very pleasant but for the flies, of which there was a very "plague," blessed with such appetites that, in addition to feasting upon the persons of our navigators, which ought to have satisfied moderate flies, they actually ate the colours off the draughtsman's drawings as fast as he laid them on.

VIEW OF TAHITI.

CHAPTER II.

Tahiti and its People.

THE island of Otaheite, or Tahiti, where Cook and his companions remained three months, is the largest of the group known as the Society Islands, lying in about the centre of the South Pacific Ocean. It is hilly, and well wooded; the soil fertile, and well watered. Its produce was found to be bread-fruit, cocoa-nuts, excellent bananas, plantains, sweet potatoes, yams, sugar-cane, with many other vegetables and fruits, which, growing of themselves, or with the least possible trouble on the part of the natives, rendered the inhabitants very lazy. Dogs, which they ate, pigs, and poultry, were among their possessions; they could have very good fish for the catching; and in this art their adroitness was remarkable, their implements singularly effective. The inhabitants were tall, and well-made, with olive complexions, dark hair, rather flat noses, and, generally, beautiful, expressive eyes. Possessing, like the rest of the world, a fair share of personal vanity, some of the more aristocratic among the men would shut themselves up for a month or two, eating bread-fruit only, and perspiring, in that hot climate, beneath a great heap of clothing, solely for the purpose of making themselves fair. The men wore their hair long, either flowing, or tied in a bunch on the top of the head, with a feather stuck upright in it. At times the hair was supplemented by a rather ludicrous wig. The women had theirs cut short. The dress of both consisted of a scanty allowance of cloth or matting of their own manufacture: the former too fragile to bear rain. For head gear, little bonnets of matting or cocoa-nut leaves were worn, made in a few minutes, as wanted, and then thrown away. The women had turbans, and head-dresses of human hair, plaited in fine strands, and wound thickly around the head. Ear-rings were used both by men and women, but in one ear only. They consisted of stone, berries, shells, pearls; but the beads of the new-comers soon drove native ornaments of this kind out of fashion. Their bodies—men and women alike—were abundantly tattooed. And, for this special decoration, "Pride must abide" might well have been taken as a motto: the various lines and devices indelibly traced upon their much-enduring skins being produced by striking into them a little instrument, shaped something like a hoe, and having teeth like a saw (only straight instead of slanting), charged with home-made lamp-black. This process of beautifying was, unluckily for the patient, a very slow one. But then the satisfaction arising from it afterwards!

The simple dwellings of these people were erected in the grateful shade of their groves of bread-fruit and cocoa-nuts; the absence of underwood in the forests rendering them airy as well as cool.

A native house of those days formed an oblong square, its ridged roof, with projecting eaves to within a few feet of the ground, being supported upon three rows of posts, one on each side, the third in the middle of the building. Palm leaves served for thatch, and the floor, strewn some inches deep with hay, over which mats were laid, was their seat by day, and their bed by night; though in some houses the master of the family had the distinguished honour of a stool all to himself. Small hollowed blocks of wood were used to support the head, as we see them in Egyptian antiquities. Dwellings on a less scale, for the sole use of a chief and his wife, were made so that they could be carried about like tents; and, instead of being open to all the breezes of heaven, were walled with cocoa-nut leaves.

As is always the case in hot countries, vegetable food was chiefly eaten by the people of Tahiti. Pork was the dish of honour here, and when a chief killed a hog, it was duly shared among his numerous attendants, whose portions were at times but small ones, by reason of the meat having to be divided among so many. The mode of dressing hog or dog was appetising. The roast, first prepared by singeing and scraping off the bristles or hair with a shell, was placed in a shallow pit, previously heated with burning wood, with which stones were placed in layers, in order to retain the heat. Some of the stones were laid beneath, others over the meat, green leaves being placed between it and them; and the whole, covered close with earth, was left for between three and four hours, when the oven was opened, and the food found excellently cooked, even to a European palate. The dogs kept for eating were fed exclusively on vegetables; and our voyagers, venturing on the experiment of a dog-dinner, thought it almost as good as lamb. The sea, which seemed almost a second home to the Tahitians, yielded them excellent fish, some of which they ate raw.

The bread-fruit, in addition to being cooked plain in the oven, in the same way as the animal food, formed the basis of several fancy dishes—a sort of pudding and custard course.

Like other people who know what is good, the natives had their sauces as well as solid food. Salt water was the leading one; those who lived at the sea-side fetching it as wanted, others in the interior keeping a supply in bamboos. One of the holiday sauces was made of cocoa-nuts beaten into a paste with sea-water: sufficiently disagreeable, one would think, but some of Cook's party got to prefer it, as a fish sauce, to any of their own.

The usual drink was water, or the milk of the cocoa-nut. Occasionally, however, the great men got terribly tipsy on *Ava*, a drink prepared from the root of a species of pepper plant. This unedifying refreshment was, fortunately, denied to the women, and generally to all but those of high degree, whose peculiar prerogative it was to make beasts of themselves. The intoxicating drinks of the English were freely, and in entire ignorance of their properties, drunk by some of their guests. But, experiencing the effect of them, they had the sense never to repeat the dose.

To have a better idea of Tahitian feeding, and table-manners—only that table they have none,—we will just look at a native gentleman of the olden time, at his ample dinner—for the quantity they ate was enormous. There he sits in the shade, with a great number of bread-fruit or banana leaves spread on the ground before him, by way of table-cloth. The materials of his meal—fish, bread-fruit, bananas, or apples—wrapped in leaves, are placed in a basket at his side, together with two cocoa-nut shells—one holding salt water, for sauce, the other fresh water, for washing and other purposes. His servants sit round him, and the ceremony begins by his washing his hands and mouth with the fresh water: a process frequently repeated during dinner-time, the natives being exceedingly clean in their habits; after which he takes a piece of bread-fruit from the basket, and, first peeling it, crams as much as possible into his mouth. Whilst working away at this, he helps himself to one of the fish, and, breaking it up into the savoury salt water, places the other fish and the remainder of the bread-fruit upon his leafy table-cloth. This done, he picks out a bit of the fish, bringing with it as much of the salt water as possible, and goes on eating it in the same fashion, varied by sips of salt water from the cocoa-nut shell or the palm of his hand, until the fish part of his dinner is ended. A servant meanwhile has, with his teeth, husked a young cocoa-nut, which, pierced with his finger, or broken with a stone, affords the great man drink. If flesh, instead of fish, has formed his dinner, a piece of bamboo, split on the spot with his nail, is used as a knife to divide it.

The next course is a cram of plantains or apples, the latter scrupulously pared with a shell picked up at random from the multitude lying about. The meal winds up with a large cocoa-nut shell of bread-fruit, beaten up into a kind of thick custard. Washing the hands and mouth succeeds; my lord has dined, and he then settles himself down to take a good sleep.

Their meals were frequent. According to the droll remark of a native, they dined three times a-day. As, in addition, they had breakfast, lunch, and supper, it must be admitted that the national house-keeping was liberal. The men and women not only ate separately, but had their food prepared apart, that of the latter being of an inferior kind: the dish of honour, pork, seldom made its appearance before them; whilst their lords banqueted also on the best quality of the plantains.

Fire, of course, was not needed, except for cooking. Their mode of procuring it was by twirling, after the manner of a drill, a pointed piece of hard wood, pressed against one of softer fibre. The rapid motion produced flame, which was caught by some species of a substitute for tinder. For candles they used an oily kind of nut; by thrusting a skewer through a number of them, which burnt by degrees, one after the other, they got a tolerable light. A Brazil nut, set alight at one end, burns like a gas jet.

The amusements of these people were simple, like themselves. A mild sort of boxing or wrestling match was one of them: their easy-going constitutions rendering them, perhaps, incapable of anything very serious in this way. Then there was shooting with bow and arrow—length of flight, not accuracy of aim, winning the prize. The Armstrongs would have been a popular clan here. In throwing the lance (a weapon about nine feet long), hitting the mark—

the stem of a young plantain, about twenty yards distant
—was the object. Another of their pastimes was a very
beautiful and exhilarating one: the slight canoe, with only
one man in it, being paddled out seaward until it met the
advancing swell, which, raising it on its broad bosom,
carried the little skiff swiftly back again to the shore. It
was there emptied of the water it had "shipped," and again
paddled out to sea, again to be borne rapidly to land upon
the heaving swell. With what a glorious swing it must
have gone in! At another of the islands of the Society
group this diversion was practised by simply clinging to a
short plank.

Music had its charms for these "savage breasts:" their
own simple melodies appearing to exercise great influence
over them. Flutes, made of a foot's length of bamboo
and drums, solid at one end (the shark's-skin cover of the
open end being beaten with the hand, instead of a drum-
stick), were the only instruments seen on this occasion.
As with ourselves, bands of strolling musicians amused the
people, extemporising the verses which were sung to the
rude accompaniment of these flutes and drums; and, as our
voyagers listened, it was found that the wonderful visitors
formed the burden of their song.

Two kinds of boats were found in use by the inhabitants of this and the neighbouring islands: one for
short voyages, flat at side and at bottom, like a narrow
trough, and of all sizes from ten to seventy feet in length
called *Ivahah;* the other, shaped much like other boats,
known as *Pahie*. The former was used for fighting
fishing, and ordinary water-travelling; the latter for long

voyages, perhaps of twenty days or so at sea, and also for fighting. The Ivahah, for war purposes, had its head and stern, more especially the latter, curved high above the body of the boat; and, here, "perched up aloft," sat a big lad, whose use was not clearly made out, but it was supposed he had something to do as assistant to one who directed the movements of the vessel. Two of them were lashed together, about three feet apart, and a stage being erected upon the platform thus obtained, was the point of vantage for the warriors, who thence slung stones, and darted their spears at the enemy. The rowers were placed beneath this stage, as were also fresh reserves of fighting-men to take the place of the killed and wounded. The Ivahah, for travelling, was always double, with a small house, on a stage like that of the sea-boats, for its occupants. The fishing Ivahah was rarely thus arranged. Masts and sails of a not very elaborate kind were used for both. The paddles for rowing had long handles, with broad, flat blades, and were wielded with such good will as to shoot the vessel rapidly on its course. The boats, owing to their construction, were leaky. Their length, together with the height of the head and stern, rendered them easy to launch or land through the surf.

The only tools possessed by the natives for boat-building, house-building, felling timber, and all other mechanical work, were a stone adze, a chisel or gouge of bone, a coarse file of coral, and a fine one of ray-skin, used with coral sand. The adze varied in weight from six or eight pounds, to a few ounces; the former being for rough, the latter for fine work and carving. For the chisel,

ARMS AND INSTRUMENTS—SOCIETY ISLANDS.

a man's arm-bone, one of those between the wrist and the elbow, was preferred. Not one morsel of iron had they. No wonder the poor creatures could not help stealing nails and hatchets, when they came in their way.

Our illustration groups a number of native arms and instruments of the Society Islands: adzes of various sizes, the head strongly bound to the handle; long, slender harpoons for striking fish; a lance head; chisel; tools for tattooing—one would not like an hour's tapping of those teeth into one's skin; flutes, and what looks like Pandean pipes; truncheon, with loop to secure it to the wrist; and the instrument used for pounding bread-fruit.

The felling of a tree, of, perhaps, eight feet in girth, was a work of labour as well as of skill, with these miserable stone adzes; many days, and many hands, were required for it. But "little strokes fell great oaks," and so it was done at last. When down, it was split into planks, three or four inches thick, the whole length of the trunk, often forty feet to the branches, these planks being afterwards smoothed with the adzes. As they had no means of bending timber, everything had to be shaped by hand, scooped, and hollowed, and shaved away, as required. Oh, the infinite labour and patience required for such work! We, for whom almost everything is done by machinery, can scarcely form an idea of it. The timber of the bread-fruit tree was more easily wrought than that of others, and this sufficed for their smaller boats.

The native cloth was, more properly speaking, felt; for, having no machinery for weaving, it was prepared after the manner of the latter, that is, by pressure.

The material worked up was the inner bark of three different kinds of trees, all of which were carefully cultivated for the purpose. The Paper Mulberry supplied the finest kind, worn by the principal people. The Bread-fruit furnished a harsher sort, for common use. A species of Wild Fig yielded a cloth, coarse and harsh, of a dark brown colour; but this was really the most valuable of 'all, as it was impervious to water, which the others were not. This kind was usually perfumed, and reserved for the morning dress of chiefs.

The process of making or felting was the same in all cases. The bark, being stripped from the tree, was steeped, like our flax, in a running stream. It was secured with stones to prevent its being carried away. When it was sufficiently softened, the women, sitting down in the water, with the steeped bark laid, inner side down, on a smooth piece of wood, scraped off the green outside with a shell. Having scraped until nothing but the fine interior fibres remained, these were spread out on plantain leaves, in layers, so as to make a mat of equal thickness, and left until morning, by which time the whole adhered so as to be removed in one piece. This was placed upon a board of suitable size, and beaten with mallets, one foot long and three inches thick: the four faces of these tools being grooved in various degrees of fineness. The side with the largest groove was first applied, the felt spreading very much beneath its strokes, which descended with the regularity of a smith's hammer on the anvil. The other sides succeeded in their turn; and the result, after all the hammering and pounding, was cloth—that is, felt—which, in some instances, after more prolonged treatment, was almost as thin as muslin.

The cloth was capable of being washed when soiled, the process being similar to that of the making of it—steeping and beating. It was softer and whiter after being washed. The edges of the thin cloth, and one side of the thicker fabric, were dyed a vivid scarlet and bright yellow, with the juice of vegetables; and one may imagine the striking effect, in that sunny climate, of these rich hues, contrasting with the pure white of the rest of the fabric.

The mats in common use were woven with great skill and rapidity, and were used, according to their different kinds of coarse and fine, either for bed and seats, or for clothing. Baskets of cocoa-nut leaves cost these ingenious folks but a few minutes' work of their rapid fingers. Ropes and lines, of all sorts and sizes, and for all sorts of purposes, were equally well constructed. Of the finer ones good fishing-nets were made. A large net, of the kind called Seine-net, was made of cocoa-nut leaves, loosely interwoven.

Nets and lines were not, however, the sole Tahitian means of taking fish: they harpooned them with singular dexterity. The harpoon was of cane, pointed with hard wood.

CHAPTER III.

Huaheine, Ulietea, and other of the Society Islands— New Zealand.

COOK'S astronomical work being successfully accomplished, he weighed anchor July 13, 1769, and sailed from Otaheite, after a stay there of three months. He left amid a chorus of lamentations from his simple friends: lamentations that were well deserved, for his mission was not only a geographical and scientific one, but one of beneficence also; for here, as well as in each out-of-the-way place visited by him in the course of the three voyages round the world that have made his name famous and honourable, he left behind him useful animals—horses, oxen, sheep, poultry, previouly unknown in the island—or planted seeds of equally useful vegetables.

Before finally breaking up his camp, not only were large quantities of seeds of water-melons, oranges, and lemons, given to the natives, who were thankful for them, but Mr. Banks planted some himself, as well as various trees and plants from Rio, in ground specially prepared near the fort. Seeds had been taken out from England, but on opening the cases it was found that nearly the half of

HOUSE OF WORSHIP, HUAHINE.

their contents had perished; for it is still one of the problems of modern times, safely to transmit to and reproduce in one clime the good things of another.

It should be mentioned that the name of this island, Otaheite—or, as we now call it, Tahiti—was not known before Cook's visit. It was on the 10th of May that he learned it from the natives. It had before this been known in England as King George the Third's Island, so named by Captain Wallis.

But in addition to leaving something behind him, Cook brought something away from Otaheite. One of the natives, a man of high rank and considerable intelligence, who had been much with the voyagers during their stay, took it into his head to accompany his new friends on their departure, and was willingly received on board the "Endeavour." Tears being the order of the day in Tahiti, poor Tupia—that was his name—took to weeping like the rest, as the ship took her slow way from the surf-girt shores; but did his best to hide it.

Fine weather and favourable winds carried our enterprising mariners to Huaheine, one of the Society Islands group, but hitherto unknown to Europeans. It is about thirty-one leagues from Tahiti, and lies somewhat north-west of it. It is small, being only between twenty-two and twenty-three miles in circuit. The surface is diversified, and it has a good harbour. The king received his visitors with much kindness, and, as a proof of friendship, begged to exchange names with Cook, who, for the remainder of his stay, was, accordingly, Oree, whilst, for the same period, his majesty accommodated his new acquaintance's name to his own language by becoming Cookee. There was a tendency among the people of this group to add a sound, generally an *e*, to the end of the words learned by them from their English visitors.

The people of Huaheine were evidently cousins-german to those of Tahiti, with the exception—as Tupia affirmed —of their not being thieves. In this particular Tupia was mistaken, for presently one of them was caught in the very act of helping himself to his neighbour's goods. But as his own friends, after inquiring into the merits of the case, prescribed for him a good beating, which was administered on the spot, their morality on this point must still be commended. They proved exceedingly cautious traders: every article offered them for sale requiring the opinion of twenty or thirty bystanders before any one ventured to bid for it.

The seasons appeared to be earlier here than in Tahiti. Of the cocoa-nut—one of the prime blessings of these southern isles—a pleasant food was made by shredding the meat fine, mixing it with yams treated in the same manner, and then baking the compound with hot stones. That sounds as if it ought to be good. The men were big and stout, but exceedingly idle. The delicate creatures, six feet high, and broad in proportion, declined ascending the hills with their active visitors, on the plea that the fatigue would kill them! Before sailing, the commander, in commemoration of his having discovered the island, gave his friend Cookee a farewell token. It was a piece of pewter, on which was impressed :—" His Britannic Majesty's ship ' Endeavour,' Lieutenant Cook, Commander, 16th July, 1769, Huaheine." A pleased and proud man was the small monarch on receiving this flattering gift, together with other presents; and the two parted in high good humour.

A cruise of three weeks in and out and about the principal islands, afforded variety of adventures, and at one of them, Ulietea, where they met with very good treatment, they were entertained by a kind of Merry Andrew, who, wearing an extraordinary head-dress of wicker-work, about four feet high, adorned with feathers and sharks' teeth, jumped and danced before them: the fun of the thing being that in the course of his gyrations he occasionally brought his stupendous head-gear so near the faces of the spectators as to make them jump. A roar of laughter applauded this part of the performance whenever it took place, more especially if some European suddenly drew back, to avoid an expected *whack* with the top-heavy basket-work. Fresh meat and vegetables were also obtained: not unacceptable when the ship's bread—biscuit, that is—was in such a state that the maggots in it burnt their mouths like mustard.

To the islands of this group Cook gave the collective name of the Society Islands, in honour of the Royal Society of England, which had done much to foster discovery as well as science: leaving to each one its native name.

A four days' run southwards brought our navigators, on the 13th August, within sight of an island which their friend Tupia informed them was called Oheteroa. On preparing to land here they met with a brisk reception. Mr. Gore was in command of the pinnace, and with him were Mr. Banks, Dr. Solander, and Tupia. The natives—

there were about sixty of them, stout, well-made savages, with a larger allowance of dress than had generally been seen among the islanders, and that of very gay colours— were armed with lances and clubs. All sat down upon the shore except two, who, as the boat skirted the beach, walked alongside of her for a while, and then attempted to swim to her. Several others, in turn, did this, but did not manage to get on board. On rounding a point, another armed body was seen, and a canoe put off to meet the advancing boat, when a sprightly attempt to seize her was made by the savages; nor was it until a couple of muskets had been fired over their heads, that they leaped into the water, and made off as fast as they could. When they regained the shore, it was evident that an eager consultation about this strange adventure took place; and the result was, that first one and then another of the natives came dancing along the shore, each brandishing his lance and uttering shouts of defiance. The two were presently joined by an old man, who, hailing the boat, asked who they were, and whence. Tupia answered them in their own language, upon which they went quietly along the beach until they joined a little group of their friends, when, after some talk, they all betook themselves to their prayers, in which Tupia joined from the boat. A little trading followed; but as it was not thought desirable to make any further acquaintance with such combative folk, the "Endeavour" continued her course southward, in the hope of finding a continent, believed, in those days, to be discoverable somewhere in the wide southern seas, but which Cook's exploring of them proved to have no existence. To the learned, this supposed continent was known as the *Terra Australis Incognita;* which may be translated —for the benefit of boys who are not "Latiners"—the unknown southern land. It was at that time thought that such a mass of land near the South Pole was requisite to balance the great northern continents.

The 25th of August, being the anniversary of the sailing of the expedition, was celebrated with Cheshire cheese and a barrel of porter, which fortunately proved excellent.

On the 6th October there was a joyful cry of "Land!" from the mast-head; and next day, ranges of hills being seen, with an enormous mountain-chain rising above them, all felt sure that this *must* be the hitherto unknown land. It proved to be the island of New Zealand, originally discovered by the Dutchman, Abel Tasman, and now to be explored by the great English navigator: little thinking that, in less than a century, its valleys should be the settled home, with shops, and streets, and squares, and railroads, of thousands of his own countrymen.

The first coming together of Englishman and New Zealander was significant. On the approach of the ship the natives at once showed fight; and when the boat went ashore, on the 7th, so determined an attempt was made to cut her off, that musket after musket had to be fired over their heads; and this not deterring them, a third shot took fatal effect upon one who was darting his lance at the boat. His friends tried to carry off their dead comrade, but soon dropped him in their hasty flight; and the English, having had quite enough of it for the time, returned on board.

Next morning, a similar attempt to open friendly negotiations failed in a similar manner. A musket shot had to be fired, and, as before, with fatal effect, before the bold attacks of these indomitable people could be put an end to. And, finding nothing was to be had at this particular spot, not even fresh water (for the river was salt), the boats withdrew to seek a better landing. This proved not a bit better,—nay, rather worse, for the surf made getting on shore impossible; and having fired over a canoe, in hope of bringing it to, they were so fiercely set upon with canoe-paddles, stones, and anything else offensive that came handy, that again the only protection was a discharge of fire-arms, which, much to the regret of the humane commander, destroyed four of their assailants. It was a bad beginning, and Cook greatly regretted that he had not let them alone. Three New Zealand lads, who had leaped out of their canoe into the water, to escape by swimming, were with difficulty got into the boat. The eldest was a most desperate young savage, and fought "like mad" to get away. When got on board, they evidently expected to be put to death immediately. As, however, instead of this, they had clothing given them, and were treated with all evidence of kindliness, their feelings underwent a rapid change, and, in high spirits, they ate heartily of the various kinds of food set before them, salt pork being most to their taste. Their appetite for supper was not at all impaired by their abundant dinner; their cram of solids at the last meal being washed down with more than a quart of water. Filled thus with "food and gladness," they were put comfortably to bed. In the course of the night, however, their low spirits returned. upon which

Tupia good-naturedly got up, and comforted them so effectually that they betook themselves to singing some of their native songs. The melody was slow, solemn, and hymn-like, with, strange to say, many semi-tones: semi-tones being usually considered peculiar to modern civilisation.

In the morning, after a heavy breakfast, the boys, bedizened with trinkets to their hearts' content, were taken ashore. But they were not, it appeared, to be so easily got rid of. Hostile demonstrations on the part of the islanders (who, they said, were their enemies, and would kill and eat them), made them again cling to their foreign protectors, who could not refuse the confidence of these lads. And so things went on for a while, backwards and forwards, the boys being eventually left on shore, much against their will.

The kind treatment these young islanders had met with was not, however, without its good effect. The commander had feared that some harm might come to them from their fierce anti-English friends. Not only was this fear disappointed, but it was found that the good report given by them of their treatment by the strangers, and of the marvels to be seen in the large floating house which had brought them from far-distant lands, had been such as to induce some of their friends to visit the latter with more peaceable intentions than had at first influenced their truly pugnacious souls. Indeed, as it afterwards turned out that the English had been suspected of man-eating, the hostility of the natives was not to be wondered at. However much a New Zealander might like to eat a man, he could not be expected to like being eaten himself.

This unfortunate spot, where Cook and his companions got nothing but fighting, except a little wood, was called by them Poverty Bay. It is to be hoped their giving it this ugly name relieved their feelings, after all the vexations they had suffered there. The natives called it Taoneroa; and it was not in itself a bad place, its low sandy shore speedily giving way to luxuriant, well-wooded hills and valleys. The south-west point of the bay was named Young Nick's Head, in honour of the lad, Nicholas Young, who first saw land.

CHAPTER IV.

Explorations of New Zealand.—Its People.

NEARLY six months were spent in sailing about, and exploring New Zealand. All our knowledge of uncivilised countries, it must be remembered, has to be got by this slow, painful process of exploration; we must make out everything for ourselves. It is not as with civilised parts of the world, where the natives can always tell us a good deal of what we want to know. And by this diligent examination Cook rendered it certain that the country consisted of islands, instead of being, as previously supposed, part of a continent. He only became acquainted with the two larger islands, the northern and the middle one; the small southern island was taken by him to be a portion of the latter. In these excursions the commander made himself well acquainted with the manners and customs of the inhabitants, who, superior in vigour to those of the Society Islands, were not equal to them in their social qualities. Fierce, combative, murderous man-eaters they proved; and the stain does not seem worn out, even in this day. Their very vigour of character doubtless makes them less easily take the impression of the civilisation around them; but if they should ever receive it thoroughly they may be expected to retain it, and turn it to better account than their soft, ductile neighbours of Tahiti, who are not so much the better for it as might have been hoped. The New Zealander is worth taming, if you can only do it thoroughly. Strange to say, these clever fellows were utterly ignorant of the value of iron; nails, so eagerly sought in the Society Islands, were not of the slightest value to them: any paltry article was more useful as purchase money for their goods than they were.

The untiring eagerness of these people to attack the new comers was again seen when the ship, in the course of her coasting voyage round the island, was in some danger, owing to the rapidly-varying depth of the water, as shown by the soundings, which at one cast would be eleven fathoms, the next seven. What are called "soundings" are measures of the depth of the sea, made by letting down a line to which a weight is fastened in order to sink it. The provoking savages sat in crowds upon the cliffs overlooking the scene, and as soon as, from some hurry and confusion on board, they judged the strangers to be in trouble, down they jumped, and tumbled hastily but well armed into their large canoes, five of which soon came almost alongside, full of excited warriors, whose gestures and nervously-handled lances showed that they meant mischief, if there was only a chance for it. A musket discharged over their heads proved useless, so grape shot was tried next; and, though it was humanely directed wide of them, it was effectual, by its splash, and splutter, and roar, in leading them to paddle quietly back again.

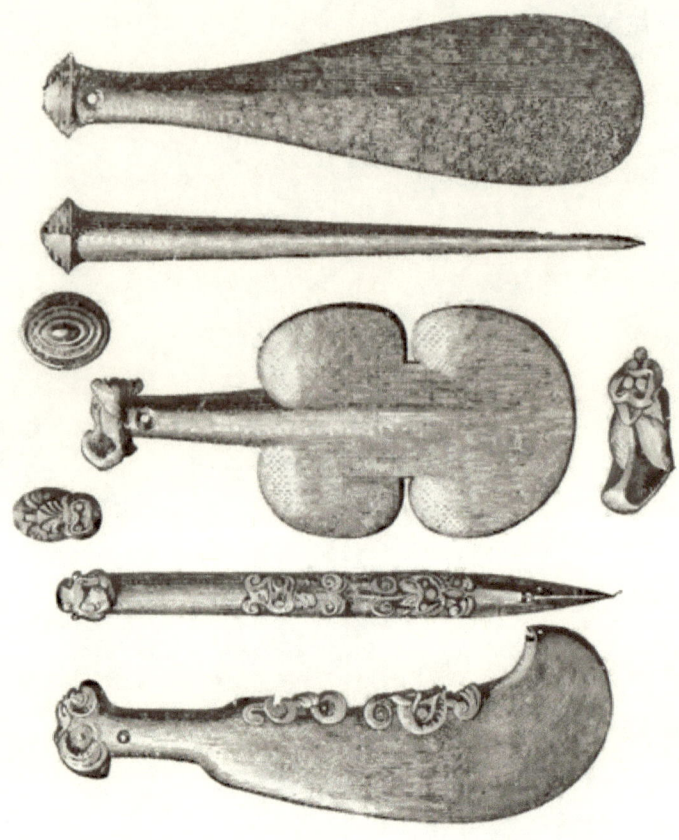

PATOO-PATOOS. NEW ZEALAND.

Spite of this admonition, the "Endeavour," in her varying course, seeking a harbour and finding none, was fallen in with by a large canoe, whose eighteen or twenty occupants, not being able to get near enough to exchange blows, contented themselves with defiant shouts, insulting gestures, and much harmless brandishing of their weapons. These weapons were very offensive weapons indeed. The lances, business-like, serviceable letters-out of life; the *patoo-patoo*, a substitute for our heavy cavalry sword, or the old battle-axe, was variously shaped of green talc, and it was quite equal to splitting a man's skull open at a blow. An occasional dose of grape shot, spattering far and wide in the water, doing these troublesome creatures no more harm than that of frightening them out of their wits, was, indeed, indispensable for opening anything like negotiations with them. Cook did not like cannonading them into friendliness, but he could not help himself; and after a couple of administrations of the kind, some fishing-boats ventured to come up and trade with the visitors amicably in—in fact, stale fish!—an article not in itself objectionable to New Zealanders, even of more recent times. Of course, rubbish like that was of no use to the commander; but he bought it, nevertheless, as a mode of obtaining their confidence. When the vendors of this valuable commodity had been well contented with their bargain, up paddled a canoe full of armed men, one of whom, clad in the furry skin of some black animal, had a piece of red baize offered him in exchange for it. He readily took the price, for English cloth was much esteemed by them; but, refusing to part with his fur until the baize was in his possession, no sooner had

he got hold of the latter than he coolly packed up both and
paddled away. This was too bad, but there was no help
for it; and, emboldened by impunity, the fishermen in
another native vessel trading at the ship's side, suddenly
seized Tayeto, a little Tahitian boy belonging to Tupia,
as he stood handing up the purchased goods, dragged him
into their canoe, and at once made off, with all haste, for
the shore. This could not be borne; the marines, who
were drawn up on deck, received orders to fire; and as
their shot dropped one man, the rest thought it wise to
let the poor boy go. Into the water he tumbled—the
Tahitians swam like fish—and, under fire from the ship
to keep off his pursuers, the little fellow got on board
unharmed, save for being almost frightened to death.

To the cape—noticeable for the tall white cliffs that
appeared to guard it—off which this miserable affair took
place, Cook gave the very appropriate name of *Kidnappers'*
Cape. The poor heathen lad thus rescued, solemnly vowed
a fish as a thank-offering to his god or guardian spirit;
and, under the enlightened direction of his master Tupia,
threw the same into the sea by way of completing the
sacrifice.

A short cruise further south being still unsatisfactory as
to finding a safe harbour, Cook tacked and turned about in
an opposite direction, bestowing upon the headland that
marked his change of course the name of Cape Turnagain.
The coast between this point and that of Cape Kidnappers
had an English-like appearance; and from the villages
discernible, not only in the valleys, but on the slopes and
crests of the hills, appeared to be well peopled.

The 18th October brought them from shore so friendly a canoe-load of chiefs and their servants as to prove rather embarrassing, seeing their visitors expressed a polite though firm intention of remaining on board all night. It was doubtless very gratifying, after all the skirmishing and some killing that had gone on, to find that these chiefs had such entire reliance upon the honour of those who had done it; but it was also perplexing, as the ship could not stand still all night to accommodate the confiding savages, who would expect to be returned safe and sound next morning on their own hearth-stones—if one may use such a phrase. They could not, however, be turned out by force, and sent packing; so, to meet the difficulty, they and their servants, canoe and all, were hoisted on board for the night. They proved well-behaved, gentlemanly men—a gentleman is not a thing of either civilisation or fashion— showing an intelligent curiosity about the various strange things that met their wondering eyes, and accepting little gifts with courtesy and gratitude. The manner both of giving and receiving, is a fine test of the stuff that is in a man. Food they would not venture upon; but their servants did double duty for their masters in this respect.

Anchoring in a newly-discovered bay, that of Tegado, on the 19th, our English had an opportunity of seeing more of the natives, and under less unfavourable circumstances, than had been the case previously. A number of canoes came off to the ship in friendly fashion; and two chiefs, dressed in jackets, one ornamented with dog's skin, and the other stuck nearly all over with tufts of red feathers, readily came on board when invited to do so. To each were given some yards of linen cloth and a spike-nail, the latter being, as was said before, not at all appreciated. They willingly trusted themselves in the boat with the commander, who, with an armed crew, went ashore to seek fresh water; but the violence of the surf preventing any landing, they signalled to their own people for a canoe—canoes can live in any kind of uproarious sea—and went off, promising supplies of fish and sweet potatoes; the latter being one of the products of the country, and not so well liked by Europeans as our own naturalised sort.

Managing to land in the evening, a kindly reception was had; and as fresh water was found, it was determined to remain here to refill the casks.

The company which went ashore on the 21st, though a strong one, did not excite any apprehension or alarm on the part of the natives, who went quietly about their own business, at meal-time each returning to his hut for dinner, as though no strangers were at hand. Fish, with roasted fern-root in place of bread, seemed to be their diet at this season. Their provision grounds, of from one or two acres to ten, were well and regularly laid out, and closely fenced with reeds. The ground was turned up with a long, sharp-ended stake, which served alike as plough and spade in the light soil of the country.

The women were not pretty, and their ugliness was enhanced by fresh daubs of red ochre and oil. The men were less highly decorated, with the exception of one "dressy" gentleman, who, being done all over, body and clothes, with dry ochre, kept a bit of it in his hand, with which he renewed the paint as fast as it rubbed off, either

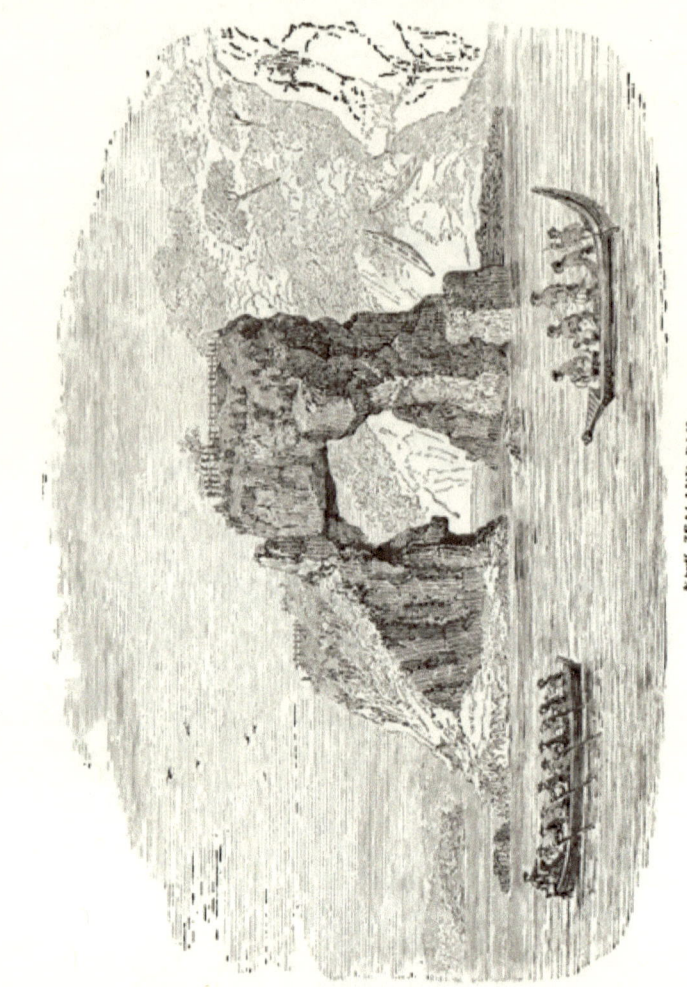
NEW ZEALAND PAH.

from his matting dress or tattooed face. The watering-party had to return to their ship in a native canoe; but, being exceedingly clumsy in "trimming" it—the canoes were simply tree-trunks, hollowed out by fire—went, souse, into the water. Their friends, after this experience of the unmanageableness of their cargo, were good enough to take them in two loads: by this means, finally getting them aboard as dry goods.

In the vicinity of the bay various excursions were made on shore, for water or for scientific purposes: each one adding to their knowledge of the country and its people. The result was satisfactory in the main; but guns, great or little, were obliged to be employed occasionally. On one occasion, three wretched canoe-loads of nearly naked savages came alongside, singing songs of defiance; and when a kindly sailor, to propitiate them, threw out a rope, thinking they wished to come on board, they just darted a lance at him by way of return. That, missing its mark, was followed by another, launched, with impetuous rage, into the ship. This was the sublimity of impudence. A musket shot over their heads was an answer they could understand, and it quickly sent them to the right about.

In more recent contests with the natives, much, and that of a very sad kind, has been heard of the New Zealand *Pah*. The first specimen of this native fortification that Cook saw, in November, 1769, impressed him by its strength, and the excellence of its construction. It was in ruins, but enough was left to show that the military architects and engineers of that savage people thoroughly understood their business. The pah—Cook calls it *heppah*

—was situated on a bold cliff, projecting into a river that emptied itself into one of the numerous bays with which the coast was indented. Rising thus from the water on three sides, the pah could not be attacked from that quarter. On the land side it was defended by a deep ditch, a bank, and an earthwork; the bank descended twenty-two feet from the top to the bottom of the ditch, the width of which was in due proportion, whilst a row of strong stakes had been driven into the crest of the bank, and along the outer margin of the ditch. The pah had evidently been destroyed by fire, perhaps the only possible way of ruining such formidable timber-work.

A wonderful supply of excellent oysters was found at the mouth of a river emptying itself into the bay where Cook now anchored; and which he named Mercury Bay, because he had there observed a transit of the planet Mercury over the sun. Great quantities of these being brought on board, the crew gave themselves up heartily to oyster-eating. Nor did fear of want on the morrow stay their enjoyment of this fresh food, so appetising to men condemned to batten daily on salt meats; so abundant were they, that the ship might almost have been loaded with them at a single tide. The river well deserved the name bestowed upon it by Cook—that of Oyster River.

On Sunday, the 12th November, a walk into the interior brought the voyagers to another exceedingly strong pah, which, being in good condition, showed more clearly the strength of such defences. Two of its sides were protected by the sea, the other two by stout palisades, ten feet high, with earthworks and ditches arranged, like those of the

E.

INTERIOR OF A PAH, NEW ZEALAND.

former pah, with all the skill of a military engineer. At Cook's request, two of the natives went through a "sham fight," to show their mode of attack and defence, which included a vast amount of furious dancing, in addition to the more serious spear and patoo-patoo part of the business. What extremes! Our immoveable battalions, solid blocks of men, with their very eyes all looking one way, and their hair brushed to the same angle, opposed to a troop of capering, prancing New Zealanders, flinging their arms and legs about, like so many toy harlequins whose strings were vigorously jerked by untiring hands.

A large quantity of celery was found here, and the boat, being laden with it, pulled off cheerily to the ship; for plenty of fresh vegetable food is the best protection against one of the most distressing maladies in the world—that called sea-scurvy, often brought on in those days by the continued use of salt provisions. The art of preserving meats and vegetables without salting was little known at that time. Before sailing out of the bay to continue their cruise round the islands, Cook took formal possession of it in the name of King George the Third, accompanying this act by a formal fluttering of the English colours to the New Zealand sun and breeze. Some say we have no right to do such things. The excuse is, that we do it to prevent other European nations from doing it, and so, if they like, shutting us out of countries that were first discovered by us. The date and the ship's name were also cut upon one of the trees near their watering place.

In their run from this anchorage to the Bay of Islands— so named by Cook from the great number of small islands which it embraces—they were beset, as before, with canoes full of infuriated savages, who threw stones, danced wildly, and, spite of Tupia's zealous efforts at peace-making, loudly invited them to "come out and fight." "Come on shore, and we will kill you all!" was their hospitable cry; to which they received the only possible answer—a musket shot through one of their boats, which, happily, satisfied them. A fine stream emptying itself into this bay was, from some fancied likeness to our own river, named the Thames. Stately trees shaded its banks: one of them, straight as a lance, at six feet from the ground had the enormous girth of near twenty feet. Its first branch sprang at eighty-nine feet from its root.

Some friendly trading took place here, the natives cheerfully parting with their clothing and arms; and, strangely enough, paper was the principal thing bought by them. One wonders what they wanted it for. But,—mischief again! One of the traders snatched up a minute glass from the binnacle (that is where the ship's compass is kept), whereupon Mr. Hicks, the officer in command, had him instantly tied up, and treated to a "dozen" from the boatswain's mate, who does the flogging in a man-of-war. The man's friends were at first disposed to resist this prompt punishment, but at length appeared convinced of the propriety of it: so much so, indeed, that when the boatswain's dozen was at an end, an old native, supposed to be the man's father, added to it a hearty beating from himself. After this double punishment, it was no wonder that the natives seemed rather shy about coming near the ship, and did not bring the fish they had promised.

Fair trading was not, however, their strong point. Cheating, by getting the price and then keeping back the article sold, was their favourite practice, which led to squabbles, then to small shot, winding up with the irresistible four-pounder, and round shot. One cheating fellow, having got a pair of old black trousers, with which he was making off, together with what he promised in return, was fired after with small shot, upon which he threw the unlucky garment into the sea and took himself off. Another of them received literally a *sharp* lesson from the hands of a midshipman on board, who revenged his wrongs by weighting a fishhook and line, which, when the offender was close under the ship's side, he dropped with such skill, that the hook caught the man by the back. He could not, however, "land" his strange fish: middy pulled, and native pulled against him, until the line snapped, and left the poor rogue with the hook sticking in him. A bold attempt to steal the ship's buoy might have been a serious matter had it succeeded. It was adroitly towed away while the crew were at dinner, and had been even got into the thieves' canoe, when a musket ball after it made them glad to throw it overboard. The kindliness of Cook and his officers to these poor ignorant creatures was strikingly shown when a frightened native, whose brother had just been hit with small shot in a skirmish, asked them piteously, "Will he die?" He was assured his brother would not die. Then a musket ball and some small shot were put into his hand, and he was told that those only who were wounded with the former would die: the other would soon be well. It was added, however, that if the English were attacked again they would certainly defend themselves with the killing balls. After this useful lesson, the man, with his wife and another brother, sat down in friendly mood with Cook and his friends, whose protection they had come to seek.

The justice of the commander was not a one-sided justice. Presently some of his crew robbed a native plantation, for which they were duly tied up and got a dozen lashes. One of the culprits had the impudence to say that there was no harm in robbing a native plantation, though it was very wrong for a native to steal from an Englishman. But he only got an extra half-dozen for his pains: well earned, one thinks.

The natives were in greater numbers in this bay than in any parts of the island yet visited. In leaving it for further exploration of the coast, the "Endeavour" had a narrow escape of wreck, the ship striking just as the man in the chains had called out "seventeen fathom." "Five fathom" was the next shout, showing the sharply-shelving nature of the rocky bottom, which had nearly made an end of the ship and her enterprise. Fortunately, she got no harm from this severe bump, but was speedily at home in deep water.

Various experiences of wind and weather, interesting to sailors but not to us, brought Cook and his stout crew, on the 16th of January, 1770, to a cove, called by him Queen Charlotte's Sound, where they cast anchor, and were received as usual by a stormy concourse of stone-throwing islanders, who accompanied their missiles with a due amount of dancing. But as from past experience our navigators knew that dancing was an essential alike of peaceful and hostile designs, it was impossible to make out what this particular dancing meant. As usual, it meant defiance; and, as usual, small shot had to be the peace-maker.

The ship being very foul after having been so long a time at sea, was careened here: that is, thrown partly on one side, that she might be scraped, and otherwise mended.

Going ashore a couple of miles from the place of anchorage, Cook, with his friends Banks, Solander, and Tupia, fell in with a native family preparing their dinner. A dog was being baked in the oven; but a provision basket close at hand too clearly told of the horrid custom among these people of eating human flesh. There lay the bones: there were too good anatomists among them to doubt of *what* those half-burned, half-gnawed bones had once formed a portion; and questioning the savages brought out the truth, simply and nakedly—"Yes, they had eaten the man, —an enemy, killed a few days before—and six with him." They only ate their enemies; not their dead friends. And one of the wretches made signs, to intimate to Mr. Banks what excellent eating they were: drawing one of the bones through his mouth as he spoke. The skilfully-preserved head of one of the victims was secured by Mr. Banks, though the owner appeared unwilling to part with it. But the buying and selling spirit was so strong in the natives, that afterwards, human bones, the relics of their ghastly meals, were quietly brought as articles of sale. Another of their frightful customs was also observed:

that of the women cutting their faces, arms, and legs, with shells, or a sharp piece of talc, as a sign of mourning for their dead husbands. "The dark places of the earth are full of cruelty."

The ship being at length set to rights, and their stores of wood and water recruited, preparations were made for leaving the Sound. One or two false starts were made, owing to the wind failing them; for in those days there was no steam to take the place of sails, flapping against the mast instead of curving to the breeze; and this gave an opportunity of again going on shore, where Mr. Banks and Dr. Solander met with the most favourable specimen of a New Zealand family that had yet come under their notice. It consisted of a young woman, a widow, and her son—the ten-year-old lord of the land whereon they had cut their timber—with a pretty numerous group of friends or servants, all sitting in the open air at their dinner. These treated their visitors with the utmost kindness and real politeness, giving them food, and earnestly pressing them to stay all night; which was, however, impossible, as the ship was expected to sail in the morning.

On the 6th of February, the wind was favourable, and the "Endeavour" left the Sound, to finish her cruise round the islands. She completed this in time to bid farewell to New Zealand at the cape to which Cook, in leaving, gave the name of Cape Farewell, and, on the 31st of March, turned her bows towards the west, not again touching land until her anchor was let go on the shores of Australia, or, as it was then called, New Holland.

We must add one or two things concerning the New

NEW ZEALAND FLAX.

Zealanders before we leave them. They were a good-looking, healthy people: kind and affectionate to each other, but hating their enemies with all their heart. Their houses were small, but well-built, affording good protection from the weather, about which, however, they did not seem much to care. The common dress was very strange-looking. It was composed of two pieces of coarse matting, made of the split leaves of a species of flag, which serves them for all the uses that hemp and flax serve us, and is now known as New Zealand flax. There were two kinds of this plant: one with yellow flowers, the other having them of a deep red. The ends of these slips were left sticking out on the outer side, so that it looked like a shaggy door-mat: this shag turning the rain, of which at times they had a good deal. One piece of the matting reached from the shoulders to the knees, the other was fastened round the waist, and fell to the ground; but this longer garment was only a kind of state dress. They had also cloth; not felted, as in Tahiti, but rudely woven by the hand, of the prepared fibres of the flag: to this, coloured borders of needlework were added. The men were abundantly tattooed, the women seldom marked more than the lips. Their hair was well daubed with fish or bird oil, which the better sort used fresh. As warlike weapons, the lance and patoo-patoo have been mentioned already; darts and battle-axes were also in use among them. The patoo-patoo was fastened to the wrist by a strap, like a policeman's truncheon; the chiefs wore it girded to the waist, as we do swords. Their canoes were large, well-constructed, and highly ornamented, and were paddled with great swiftness.

The singing-birds of this country, it was found, began their music a couple of hours after midnight, and continued it until sunrise, being silent for the rest of the day. Their song sounded very sweet, heard in the distance, as the ship lay at her moorings.

CHAPTER V.

New South Wales.—Narrow Escape from Wreck.—
Natives.

BOTANY BAY has a very ill sound in our ears now-a-days. It makes us think of thieves, and rogues, and rascals of all sorts, bundled out from our shores, and tossed down, to mend or grow worse, in a lovely spot at the other side of the world, as far from us as they possibly could be. The very name is soiled by the use that, until recently, we made of the place. But, in truth, Cook gave it that name on account of the great abundance and variety of the plants found in its neighbourhood.

It was within this bay, on the eastern coast of New South Wales, that, on the 27th of April, Cook cast anchor, after his voyage from New Zealand. Before coming to anchor a boat had been sent ahead to see what depth of water there was, and on its return the master, who had gone in it, reported having seen some of the inhabitants of the country, who had made signs to him to land. They were armed with lances, and a crooked weapon made of wood, about two feet and a-half long, which is now known as the *boomerang:* a convenient weapon, for, when you had knocked down your man or beast with it, it came back again to you, handy to knock down another. As the vessel slowly approached her anchorage other natives made their appearance, using threatening gestures, and brandishing their boomerangs, as though they meant to fight as soon as they got a chance. Two of these were striped all over with white paint, like a soldier's cross-belts, in front of the body, with broad stripes round the upper part of their legs. As their dusky faces were also done over with white, they must have had a very comical look.

Within half-a-mile of the anchoring ground there was a number of huts, towards which an old woman and some children—like the rest, without one atom of dress—were seen taking their way, each carrying a bundle of firewood. More children came out to meet them; some men returned from fishing; and then the whole party set to work to cook their dinner, scarcely deigning to notice the ship, though such a sight as it they had assuredly never set eyes upon before.

In the afternoon a party went ashore, having Tupia with them; but though the natives had taken so little notice of them in the morning, it was not so now. They were at once met by two of them, who had no mind that the new-comers should land there. Each was armed with a long lance, which he shook and brandished, talking loudly, but in a tongue of which even Tupia could not make out a word. Upon this the men were ordered to lie upon their oars, whilst Mr. Cook made all the friendly signs he could think of, and threw nails, and other little articles that he thought would please, to the savages, in

AUSTRALIAN NATIVES AND HUT.

order to show his peaceable intentions. But they never minded his nails, and as an attempt was made to bring the boat to land a stone was thrown at her, which brought that unfailing dose of small shot in return. The older of the two natives being struck on the legs with this, ran off; but it was only to fetch his shield, a strip of bark about three feet long and eighteen inches broad, to cover himself whilst he threw a lance at the English, who, by this time, had landed. His companion did the same, but, fortunately, no one was hurt, and a third musket shot drove them away, after throwing one more lance. The party at once went to the huts, and, peering in, saw the children hiding themselves behind a shield and some bark. But as the poor little frightened things did not see them, they were kindly left undisturbed: some beads and other trifles being thrown into the hut, which it was hoped might show the older natives, when they came back, that their visitors meant no harm to them.

The huts of the natives were wretched concerns, made with twigs, the two ends of which being stuck in the ground, arched over head; this roof, if it deserves such a name, having a kind of thatch of bark and palm leaves. A hole was left at one end for a door, and the fire was kindled on the ground at the opposite end. Huts still slighter than these were afterwards seen.

Some miserable canoes were drawn up on the beach. They were each made simply of the bark of one tree, tied together at the ends, the centre being kept open by sticks placed cross-wise—as children make a boat of a pea-husk. Water was an object of search here, and as none was to be found, the party returned on board, taking with them a bundle of lances dropped by one of the fighting fellows. These lances were ugly tools for hurting a man—six to fifteen feet long, and headed with four prongs having extremely sharp points of fish-bone. It was thought that they were poisoned, but that proved to be a mistake.

The first introduction of our voyagers to the New Hollanders was certainly as discouraging as that to the New Zealanders. When they went ashore next morning, they found the natives had been too frightened to come back to their huts, for there lay the beads and the other fine things, untouched, just where they had been left. Some of the people were seen by Cook in the distance, but they ran away immediately, leaving their fires, with shell-fish roasting on them. Water-casks had been brought on shore to be refilled, and these being found by a small party of natives, were curiously examined whilst the watering party were on board at their dinner. They did them no injury, and presently went away, taking with them the canoes that lay upon the beach. There was no getting a friendly meeting with them.

Two or three days after, one of the sailors died. He was taken on shore for burial, near the watering place; and the south point of the bay, where he was laid, was, in memory of him, named Sutherland Point. An excursion into the country was then made by Cook, Banks, and others, going first to the huts, where, though they found their presents still lying about unheeded, they added others to them,—looking-glasses, combs, and beads,—in hopes somebody would find them, and be kindly disposed to the givers. Never were more pains taken to win over savages, and, so far, with so little success. The country, as they advanced, was pleasantly varied with wood and grass land, though the soil was either sand or swamp. The trees, among whose branches were great numbers of beautiful birds, stood at some distance from each other, the ground between them being covered with grass, growing in tufts. Though there were many huts about, only one native was seen, who took to his heels at the first sight of white strangers. There is no doubt that the complexion of the English added to the terrors inspired by their being strangers; for amongst blacks the devil is painted white, as we whites have been in the habit of painting him black: as though colour had anything to do with wickedness! Mr. Gore, the lieutenant, who had been employed on other duty, as soon as his work was done, took boat to the shore, with only one person, a midshipman, with him. He sent the boat back as soon as they had landed, and then the two set out to find the watering party. They soon fell in with a well-armed lot of natives, who, fortunately for Mr. Gore and his companion, contented themselves with dogging the strangers until they reached their comrades. Another officer, seeing the natives had halted, and were standing quietly at a little distance, took it into his foolish head to go, along with two or three as foolish as himself, towards them. But, alas! as the courageous little party drew near to the squad of dusky faces, their valour suddenly "oozed out at the palms of their hands;" in a fright they wheeled round, and went back again as fast as they could. This appearance of fear was quite enough to invite an attack from the savages, four of whom sprang forward, and launched their spears at the rapidly-retreating heroes with such force that, in their whizzing flight of forty yards, they went beyond the mark at which they were aimed. It was well those natives were bad shots, otherwise such vigorous lancers might have *spitted* the doughty Mr. Monkhouse and his men. This striking demonstration luckily satisfied the assailants, and they drew off, leaving the men, who were getting water, to return to their ship in peace. Cook was a strict disciplinarian, as all good commanders are; and we can imagine how that officer would "catch it" when he got on board.

A number of other excursions were made into the country whilst the "Endeavour" lay here, but nothing could be done towards making friends with the people. The neighbourhood was, however, an admirable one for botanising; and Mr. Banks, with his friend, Dr. Solander, enjoyed themselves to their hearts' content in examining the wonderful and abundant vegetation around this part of the coast.

On the 6th May, Cook weighed anchor, and sailed north along the coast, passing, at the distance of ten miles, another fine bay, which he named Port Jackson; on whose northern shore now stands Sydney, the fine capital of New South Wales. Other bays, capes, and points, were also named by him as he pursued this course; the names being selected either as expressive of some feature of the place to which it was given, as Broken Bay, from the broken character of the land; to commemorate some notable person, as Cape Hawke, after the Admiral Lord Hawke; or

PORT JACKSON, BOTANY BAY.

some circumstance connected with it, as Cape Tribulation, from Cook's narrow escape from shipwreck off that cape. The country was found more hilly as he went north.

His next anchorage was in a bay with a fine sandy bottom, the wind blowing so cold that cloaks had to be called for, for the trip to land. The soil at this part was much worse than about Botany Bay. Among the trees seen by Cook's party was the mangrove, which loves a salt, swampy ground. It was the first they had seen in this country. Its branches abounded with the nest of a green stinging ant, that bit savagely when disturbed; and with green caterpillars, whose hairs stung like nettles, only very much worse, but the pain did not last so long as that of the nettle sting. A large bustard, weighing seventeen pounds, was shot in the course of the morning, and as it afforded them an excellent dinner, out of gratitude to its memory the inlet was named after it, Bustard Bay. Great plenty of fish and oysters might have been had in the bay, but, as ill luck would have it, they tore the net all to pieces at the first haul.

Meanwhile, not a creature was seen, though several fires still burning, with shells, fish-bones, and other fragments scattered about, showed that natives could not be far off, though they contrived to hide themselves so thoroughly. But as there was not the least trace of hut, or dwelling of any sort, Tupia, with an air of mild superiority, called the people "poor wretches." Those left on board said that during the absence of the commander about twenty of the natives had come down to the beach, stared at the ship, and then gone their way.

On the 26th of May, some days after leaving Bustard Bay, the ship was suddenly found in shoal water, and they were at once obliged to anchor in sixteen feet, only two feet more than she drew. In this awkward position, Mr. Banks amused himself by fishing, with hook and line, out of the cabin window. Among his catches were two remarkable crabs: one of them with claws and joints of the most beautiful ultramarine, whilst the under part of its body was an exquisite shining white, like old china; the other had three brown spots on his back, with the joints and ends of the legs touched up with the same beautiful blue.

Anchoring again on the 28th, two miles from land, Cook, Mr. Banks, and others went on shore to see if they could find a suitable spot for again careening the ship, which was in a very bad state. The ground here was covered with a grass whose bearded seeds not only stuck in their clothes, but worked their way through to the skin in a most annoying manner, whilst all around the air swarmed with musquitoes and millions of butterflies. Large ants' nests—the size of a bushel measure—made of clay, were seen on some of the trees. Others were taken possession of by black ants, who picked all the pith out of the branches, even to the smallest twigs, and then lived in the hollow part. The breaking off of one of these ant-inhabited boughs (which gave no outward signs of their strange occupancy) was rather an awkward matter, as the disturbed and angry insects poured out in thousands, and revenged their wrongs by the multitude and venom of their stings. In the course of this walk a very queer fish was also found, that used its breast fins like legs, and leaped in and out of the water.

and on dry land, as it pleased. Surely these were marvels enough for one day. But as no water was to be found, it was not a suitable place for laying up the ship. Naming it, from this circumstance, Thirsty Sound, they sailed again on the 31st.

Coasting is always dangerous, and more especially so along the shores of New Holland, owing to hidden shoals running out into the sea; and rocks uprising, needle-like, high and sharp, from the bed of the ocean. The navigation had so far been safe; but on the 10th of June, on a clear, moonlight light, and with a fine breeze, the "Endeavour" struck, and stuck fast, save that the heaving waters continued to beat her on the craggy rock on which she lay, with such violence that those on board could scarce keep their legs. Instantly every one was on deck; the sails were taken in, and boats were lowered, in order that the exact position of the vessel might be ascertained. It was bad enough, for the sea had carried her over a ledge of rock; and now she was lying, beating her timbers to smash, in a hollow on the surface of it, where the water varied in depth from two or three to eighteen or twenty-four feet. To take her back again over that ledge seemed impossible; their utmost efforts, with anchors and cables all a-strain, failed to move her: bump, bump, bump went she, until her sheathing and false keel were knocked off, and seen floating in fragments around them. This was terrible; lightening her was the only thing that could be done, and, immediately, overboard went guns, ballast, casks, hoop staves, oil-jars, old stores, every article that could by possibility lessen the weight of the ship: not only to stop that dreadful bumping which was beating her to bits, but to afford a chance of getting her over the ledge into deep water. The ebbing tide had somewhat abated the violence of her continual striking, by allowing her to settle closer on her rocky bed; but tides that ebb also flow, and the next twelve hours had to be provided for. Even the water-casks were started into the hold, and their contents speedily pumped overboard, further to diminish her weight.

Still there she lay; and when the tide rose, the leak increased so much that, spite of incessant pumping, it was to be feared that even if got off the rock, she must certainly go down; and there were not boats enough to carry all ashore, twenty miles off. Incessant labour, directed by educated skill, *did* get her off at last; but by that time, twenty-four hours of such work had so exhausted the crew, that none could take his turn at the pumps for more than a few minutes together. Worn out with that, down he dropped on deck, three or four inches deep in running water; and so on, one after another: each wearied man, sinking down for a brief rest, and then up again, to strain every muscle in a fresh spell at the pumps. Presently these gained a little upon the leak; and at that moment a midshipman—Mr. Monkhouse—proposed what is called "fothering" the vessel. This "fothering" consists in passing underneath the ship's bottom, at the place where it leaks, a sail, upon which a quantity of oakum or wool is stitched loosely down, and weighted with all the soft rubbish that comes to hand. The action of the sea presses this pad into the leak, and so, for a time, prevents the entrance of the water. No time was lost in setting about this; the prepared sail, by means of ropes, was safely got into its place—no easy task; and it acted so well, that the leakage, which had previously gained upon three pumps, was now effectually kept in check by only one. With this in their favour, the crew were at last rescued from their perilous condition, the "Endeavour" being, after many delays and much anxiety, brought into a convenient harbour on the morning of the 17th.

Tents were immediately set up on shore—a dreary, barren, salt-water-swampy kind of place. Into one of them the invalids—eight or nine men—were brought; the other was used for stores and provisions. Next morning, they set to work again upon the ship, which, by slow degrees, was thoroughly lightened of her remaining heavy contents, in order to lay her on her side to repair damages. When this was done, the nature and extent of the injury was clearly seen, and found to be of an extraordinary character. The sharp, jagged coral rock had cut through her planking, as with a knife: a clean, smooth cut, without a splinter about it. But, strange to say, one large hole, enough of itself to have sent them all to the bottom, was stopped up so effectually by a portion of the rock that had pierced it breaking off and sticking there, that, instead of the water pouring in in a flood, as it would otherwise have done, it had only gained an entrance in comparative driblets, between the inequalities of the stone and the sides of the opening made by it. This alone had saved all on board from destruction.

Whilst carpenters, smiths, and all the rest of their tribe were at work on the shattered vessel, others, who had time to look about them, explored the neighbourhood of their haven of refuge; and, truth to say, reported some wonderful adventures on their return. A strange animal had been seen, something like a greyhound, mouse-coloured, and extremely swift, which puzzled everybody, even Mr. Banks himself, who was supposed to know everything about animals and plants, and all other things included in what is called Natural History. In truth, this strange beast, which leapt like a deer, *was* a strange animal, being none other than a kangaroo, now, as it was believed, first seen by European eyes. One of the sailors, however, quite outdid the discoverers of the kangaroo; for in the course of his ramble in the woods he met with something that, by his own account, was queerer still, for he declared that, to the best of his belief, he had seen the devil, with horns and wings, creeping through the grass so slowly that, but for John's being "afear'd," as he said, he might have touched him. This hideous apparition proved to be a bat, which at that side of the world is a big creature, as well as a very ugly one—as it is all the world over. The man's fright, it must be said, had magnified the bat two or three dozenfold, for he told his comrades that it was the size of a gallon cask, whereas the poor thing was only as big as a partridge.

Vegetables were found here by the wanderers, some worthless, others good; and as their nets supplied them with fish and their guns with occasional pigeons, the invalids— some of them had been suffering from scurvy—were all the better for it. The master, too, going out one day to seek a passage for the ship—when she should be thoroughly

KANGAROOS.

tinkered up—through the innumerable shoals that lay between her and "blue water," found some cockles, so large that two men—hungry sailors, be it remembered—could not manage to eat the whole of one. Turtle were caught with a boat-hook on the same bank—they were not small, for three of them weighed 791 pounds—and everybody was thankful for these various additions to their cheer. It is all very fine for people who live at ease, and are well fed every day, to say they don't care about what they eat or drink; but set a man to live day after day upon salt pork or beef—salt horse, sailors used to call it, it was so coarse and hard—for a twelvemonth or so, and, philosophers though they may be, they will sing another sort of tune, and think a few good meals of fresh provisions something like a heaven upon earth, as these poor disease-stricken seamen did.

Still no natives could be got hold of. At length, on the 10th of July, four were seen in the distance, apparently spearing fish, and as Cook would not, for fear of frightening them, allow his people to go to them, two of the four came over in their canoe to within a musket shot of the ship. Their loud jabber, of which not one word was understood, was answered by shouts, and all the friendly signs that could be thought of. These seemed to have some influence with them, for they presently came nearer, holding up their lances, not as though they meant to strike, but simply to show that they could take care of themselves in case of need. Nails, beads, and other little things were thrown to them, of which they did not take the slightest notice; but when, at last, a small fish was tossed to them, it was greedily seized, and the two paddled away to fetch their friends, who returned with them. None of the lot now seemed in the least afraid; they were even persuaded to lay down their lances, of which each man carried two, as well as a throwing-stick to launch them; but it was plain that, like good soldiers, they did not like any one to come between themselves and their arms. The lances were pointed and barbed with fish-bones: they were most formidable weapons, and when thrown would stick fast in a tree fifty paces off. These men were of the middle size, but had very small limbs. Their skin was of a sooty brown colour, partly the effect of smoke and dirt, though altogether they were not bad looking. Of their features a notion may be had from our illustration: they are not bad faces.

They must have been satisfied with their reception, for next day three of them came again, bringing a friend. The stranger wore a bone, five or six inches long, and about the thickness of a finger, stuck through the cartilage of his nose: a fashion among New Hollanders, as it was afterwards discovered. The sailors, for fun, called this their "spritsail-yard." Not only was it frightful, it was very inconvenient also, causing them to snuffle, and keep their mouths wide open in order to breathe. Clothing they had none—none was ever worn by these people—so it was not surprising that when a piece of an old shirt was given to a native he tied it round his head like a bandage, instead of trying to put it on properly. This little party presented the white strangers with a fish, but seeing that the canoe in which they came was an object of curiosity, they took fright, jumped into it in a hurry, and paddled themselves

NATIVES OF NEW SOUTH WALES.

away. On paying another visit some fish was, at their request—by signs, of course: no one understood a word that they said—cooked for them; but after eating a bit they threw the rest to Mr. Banks' dog.

It has been said that excellent turtle were procured in the vicinity of the creek, and these seemed to be as tempting to the natives as to the English who had caught them, for on the 19th, when a pretty large party of natives came to the ship, on seeing the turtle—the only thing the English had for which they appeared to care—one of the set made signs that a turtle should be given to them. This was refused, for turtle was procured with difficulty, though it, and indeed every other article of fresh food found during the expedition, was shared equally, the commander getting no more than the common sailor; but by way of being civil, as there was no cooked meat about, some biscuit was offered him instead. Biscuit instead of turtle was too good; the fellow flung it overboard in a pet. Stamping with rage, on a fresh refusal of the much-coveted turtle, another of the set gave Mr. Banks a good push out of the way; and, finally, finding that no one would give them what they wanted, they tried to take it by force, laying hold of two of the turtle and dragging them towards their canoe. They were foiled here also; and after repeated vain attempts to help themselves, at last gave it up, jumped into their canoes, and paddled away in a fury. Their temper was not mended by their hard row, for no sooner had they landed, than in revenge they rapidly set fire to the grass around the tents. This, being five or six feet high and quite dry, blazed up furiously, destroying the smith's forge, prematurely singeing some pigs—one was burnt to death—and spreading far into the woods, until at the distance of ten miles its course was still to be traced. Mr. Banks' tent would have shared the fate of the forge, had it not been instantly dragged down to the beach. The grass was next fired where the fishing-nets and a quantity of linen were laid out to dry, so that it became absolutely necessary to stop these desperate mischief-makers by firing small shot at them. Some were hit with this, and as a ball was also sent alongside them, they thought proper to give in: returning apparently in penitent mood, for they approached unarmed, promising by signs that they would "never do so any more."

They kept their word, and were even friendly enough to put a seaman, who fell in with a party sitting round their fire, on the most direct road to his ship.

It was not until the 4th of August that the ship, being refitted as well as was possible under such circumstances, was got out of the small creek in which she had lain. To commemorate her stay there, Cook gave the name of Endeavour River to the stream running into this inlet.

But though out of harbour, the vessel was not yet at sea, and so numerous and embarrassing were the shoals and reefs on this dangerous coast, that it was the 13th of the month before she was fairly afloat in deep water. Even then they were by no means "out of the wood;" for in three days' time—such were the difficulties of navigating these hitherto unknown waters—they were only too thankful to get, with labour and pains, safely back to the very spot from which, so happily as they thought, they had, with labour and pains, made their escape. With not a breath of wind to fill the sails, rocks within a hundred yards of them whilst they were in unfathomable waters, towing by the boats and the use of "sweeps"—these are long oars for propelling large vessels—were all they had to trust to, to save them from the destruction that again seemed close upon them. Once inside the reef, it was determined to keep there, sailing within it for the remainder of their coasting voyage. Had they done otherwise, they might have been carried very wide of their mark, which now was to find out whether New Holland did or did not make a part of New Guinea. Before proceeding on this changed plan, however, it was necessary to have the pinnace put to rights, as she was much damaged. Whilst this was being done, the other boats were sent out to seek provender, and returned in the afternoon with a good cargo of shell-fish, chiefly cockles. These cockles were so large that it took a couple of men to move them, and, when cleared of the shells, there were twenty pounds of solid meat in each.

Passing thus along the coast, the eastern side of New Holland was thoroughly explored, from Cape Howe in the south, to Cape York in the north, and for the first time by Europeans. Possession for the English had been taken of particular portions of it, as one after another had been discovered; but now, when about to alter his course to sail for New Guinea (whose separation from New Holland was speedily to be ascertained), the commander took formal possession of the entire eastern portion of the island, from latitude $38°$ to $10\frac{1}{2}°$ S., for His Britannic Majesty King

George III., and under the name of New South Wales. When the colours were hoisted in honour of this formal act, three volleys were fired, answered by three volleys from the "Endeavour." The small island on the coast where this little scene was enacted, was named by Cook Possession Island.

Since that date, real possession of New Holland—or Australia—has been taken by the thousands of our countrymen who have colonised it, and made it now a portion of the vast British Empire.

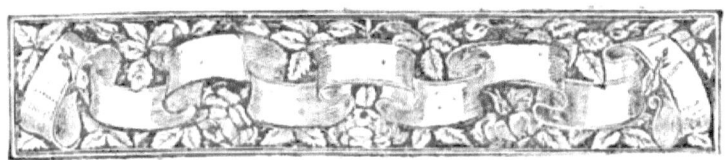

CHAPTER VI.

NEW GUINEA.—SAVU.—BATAVIA.—THE CAPE.—HOME.

ON the 23rd of October, having, by sailing through the strait that divides them, positively made out that New Holland and New Guinea were two islands instead of one, Cook bore away for the latter, amid shoals and other dangers of the sea. On the 25th, the ship had a narrow escape from striking on one of these shoals, but, by altering her course, was got into deeper water. On the 28th, the appearance of the sea made them fear that they were again among their old enemies the shoals, but, on examination, it was found that the brown tint which had alarmed them was caused by a vegetable substance unknown to the naturalists on board. The sailors, however, found a descriptive name for it, calling it sea saw-dust. At dawn of September the 3rd, the coast of New Guinea came in sight: the light morning breeze having for two days past wafted to the voyagers so strong an odour of fragrant trees and shrubs as to indicate that land could not be far off. The ship was brought to anchor three or four miles from the strand, and the commander, Mr. Banks and his servants, and Dr. Solander, all well armed, went on shore in the pinnace, the shallowness of the water compelling them to wade the last two or three hundred yards of their journey. The print of human feet on the wet sand, when they reached it, showed not only that there were inhabitants, but that they could not be very far off; so they marched along cautiously; and it was well they did so, for, as they skirted a wood, not daring to taste the cocoa-nuts that hung temptingly there, three natives suddenly bounded out of it with a hideous yell, one of them throwing from his hand something that burnt like gunpowder, but without any noise. The other two darted their lances at the intruders, who were obliged to fire instantly, in self-defence. The small shot, though it did not strike, stopped the assailants for a short space, when a third light barbed lance answered the discharge. Ball was next fired, upon which they turned, and ran swiftly away. Cook and his friends, finding the people so hostile, thought it best to return to their boat, and on their way to it saw a large body of between sixty and a hundred natives, moving towards them. The boat was, however, reached in safety, and then they were able to take a good look at the angry, shouting, naked beings before them, who kept letting off their fireworks, which appeared to be discharged from a short stick, swung sideways from them. These people were lighter coloured than the New Hollanders; but whether their skins really were so, or they were only less dirty, could not be made out. A volley of balls rattling among the trees caused them to retreat, although somewhat leisurely, and the ship was reached without more ado. Things certainly have different names, under different circumstances.

NATIVES OF NEW GUINEA.

These naked, truculent beings very likely considered their hostility patriotism, and perhaps they were right.

Some of the ship's officers were so provoked at the attack, that they would fain have persuaded the commander to send a party on shore to cut down the cocoa-nut trees, in order to procure the fruit. But as cocoa-nuts were not necessaries of life, but only luxuries, Cook would not do so unjust and cruel an act.

How much goes to the making of a good commander! Courage, fortitude, patience, justice, mercy, moderation, perseverance, self-denial: Cook seemed to possess them all.

The country hereabout appeared to be very rich and productive. Of the natives we give a specimen in our illustration. How they managed to dress their hair in that preposterous fashion, we are not told; but it was evidently a work of "labour and of skill."

The bad condition of his ship at this time induced the commander to make sail for Batavia, where, as the Dutch had long had a settlement there, he would be able to give her a thorough, civilised overhauling. Patching and mending was all that could be done on the wild shores upon which they had been cast when almost wrecked.

On his course to Batavia, Cook touched at the small and little-known island of Savu, south-west of Timor, of which at first he fancied himself the discoverer. But when, in addition to horses and flocks of sheep, a couple of men on horseback were seen having a ride on the hills, and often stopping to look at the new-comers, it was clear that, instead of more savages—of the same, or a newer pattern than those just left behind—they had fallen in with some settlement of Europeans. Mr. Gore, who was sent on shore in the pinnace, found a small group of natives of the place, who in dress and person were like Malays. They had knives stuck in their girdles, but had no other arms. They seemed friendly; but as their language was one utterly unknown to our people, much could not be made out of them. Fresh provisions, however, being much wanted for the sick, this officer was sent back again to try to procure them. On his return to the ship he brought a couple of dozen cocoa-nuts, which had been given to him as a present, the absence of the owner of the trees preventing any trading for the fruit; but he had been directed to a harbour at a little distance, where, he was told, anything that he wanted might be had. Sail was, therefore, made thither, and on hoisting the Union Jack it was replied to by a display of Dutch colours, together with a salute of three guns.

On landing here Mr. Gore was received by a guard of natives, who, carrying with them the colours that had been shown on the beach, took him at once to the rajah, or king. With the help of a Portuguese interpreter, this personage, a fat, dull man, was informed that the vessel in the bay was an English man-of-war, and that provisions were wanted for the sick on board of her. The king was quite willing to accommodate them, but as the Dutch East India Company had a settlement in the place, their agent had to be sought before leave could be had to trade with any other nation. This was readily given, and then, business being ended for the time, his majesty, with some of his retinue and the Dutch officer, expressed a wish to visit the ship. They were accordingly taken into the boat—two of the English being left behind as hostages for their safety—and got on board at two o'clock, when, as dinner was ready, the commander invited them to join himself and his officers at table. The king, a man of colour, seemed confused, and at last said frankly that he did not expect to be allowed to sit down with white men. A kindly word or two soon relieved him of this difficulty: he took his place at table, and a cheerful dinner party they made of it. As both native and Dutch potentates were present, there was nothing to hinder free permission being given to buy buffaloes, sheep, pigs, and fowls; and his majesty, having drunk quite as much wine as was good for him (and a little more), was desirous, before taking leave, of seeing the marines put through their exercise; they had been under arms to receive him. This being done, he was delighted with the precision of their movements, exclaiming, as they cocked their muskets, that "all the locks made but one click." He and his companions, well laden with presents, then went ashore, under a salute of nine guns. Mr. Banks and Dr. Solander went with their guests to the town, which contained a large number of very simply built houses, raised on short posts about four feet from the ground, and having sloping roofs thatched with palm leaves.

The fresh meat, however, was not so readily forthcoming as had been promised. But on going ashore to see about it, his majesty, in his turn, asked the English to dinner: with exquisite politeness adding, that he could scarcely think it possible they would eat food cooked by his servants. The royal dinner consisted of pork and rice, and it was served in thirty-six baskets, with the addition of three bowls of the water in which the pork had been boiled. The dishes were set out on the floor, with mats for the guests to sit upon. The hands were first washed, and then the party sat down by themselves, it not being the custom there, as they were told, for the host to sit down with the friends whom he was entertaining. The pork and rice were excellent, and even the queer broth—"pot-liquor," we should call it—was good; but the spoons, made of palm-leaves, were so small, they had scarcely patience to use them. Dinner being ended, the company went to another room to drink the wine which the English had themselves brought; the common sailors and the servants sitting down to the remains of the banquet, with a hospitable injunction, which could not be disregarded, to carry away with them what they could not eat. The gentlemen hoped that, as his majesty had so thoroughly enjoyed their wine on board ship, he might be prevailed upon to join them over it now, though he could not eat with them. But again they were disappointed; the royal excuse being that a host should never get drunk, and the only way of avoiding that was not to taste the wine.

Spite of all these civilities, it was not without a great deal of trouble, owing to the malicious meddling of the Dutch factor, that provisions were at length procured, and on reasonable terms.

The buffaloes turned out to be good eating, though there was very little meat on them considering their size. The mutton was the worst our voyagers had ever tasted, but the pork was of good quality.

The dress of the natives of Savu was of blue cotton, variously folded about the body, leaving the arms, legs, and feet bare. The men fastened their lank black hair on the top of the head with a comb, and wore either a slender fillet or a sort of small turban, of some fine fabric, either cotton or silk; the women tied theirs in a knot at the back of the head. All were excessively fond of ornaments, and a little tattooing was used both by men and women, to enrich their dark brown faces. Both men and women chewed betel and areca-nut from morning to night, which spoiled all their teeth. They sometimes mixed a little tobacco with this precious morsel. When they were not chewing, they were smoking tobacco.

The mode of cooking—wood being scarce—was precisely that lately introduced, as a novelty, into our military camp arrangements. Two holes, one small, the other larger, were dug in the earth, an opening being worked out, underground, between the two; fire was kindled in the larger one, the small serving as a draught. Holes being made in the earth over this channel, pots, shaped something like a pyramid turned upside down, instead of flat at the bottom, as usual, were inserted in them, this peculiar shape exposing a greater surface to the heat; and the contents were cooked with much less fire than would have been required had it been open to the air. One may learn something almost everywhere.

The fan-palm, whose sap produces the liquor called toddy, is a native of this island. Toddy is made by cutting the young flower-buds, and allowing the sap to drain into baskets made of the leaf of the tree. It was the common drink here, and what was not used in this way was made, by boiling, into syrup and a coarse sugar.

From Savu, 21st September, to Batavia, 9th October, the run did not afford anything of interest, except to seafaring people, to whom it is intensely interesting, and useful, too, to know in what direction the wind blows, or did blow a hundred years ago; and whether a ship had to steer to the right or to the left in working her way across the seas—though a sailor would be shocked to hear "right" or "left" spoken of in steering a ship: he would describe it by the points of the compass, of which everybody knows there are thirty-two.

When the "Endeavour" anchored in Batavia Roads, she was found to be in so unsafe a condition, that a lengthened stay was absolutely necessary. Some of her planks, indeed, were so worn away, that there was not more than the thickness of a shoe-sole between her crew and the ocean on which they floated. It was a wretched place; being sadly cheated at the hotel, where the gentlemen had to live while the ship's repairs were being carried on, was the least part of it. The climate was one of the most deadly in the world; and first one, then another, fell a victim to it. Poor Tupia, who had brightened up amazingly on their first going ashore, soon followed his little countryman and servant, Tayeto, who died on the 9th of November. He was fond of the lad, and the loss of him seemed to hasten his own end. Indeed, every one of the ship's company, Cook included, were on the sick list in this unhealthy place, except one ill-conditioned old man, between seventy and eighty years old, who ought, one thinks, to have gone first, seeing that he was drunk every day all the time of their remaining at Batavia.

Batavia then, as now, belonged to the Dutch, who in those days carried on much more extensive trading with foreign countries than they have done of late years. It is on the north side, or rather end, of the island of Java, and is so placed, that attack either by land or by sea is almost impossible; and it has a remarkably fine harbour, which makes it very valuable for shipping. But being in a low, swampy situation, and, after the manner of Dutch towns at home, pierced in all directions by canals, it was excessively unhealthy, as it continues to be to this day. Dirt reigned triumphant here—which was not after the manner of the Dutch at home, for they are exceedingly cleanly; and in so hot and damp a climate dirt is more dangerous than it is in cooler places. Before they had been on shore a week, Cook's people began to suffer, and ere the month was at an end half of them were unfit for work. The country, spite of its unhealthiness, was, however, very rich and productive, and the variety of its fruits and flowers was wonderful. The inhabitants were a mixture of Dutch, Portuguese, Chinese, and Indians, as they are called—that is, natives of Java and the islands lying around. Cook gave the name of Indians to the natives of every island visited by him during this voyage. The Chinese were here, as they seem to be everywhere, a hard-working race, and not at all particular as to what their work was. Nothing was too dirty nor too dishonest (provided it did not risk their necks) for them to undertake. And when their work was done they played with equal diligence; so that in Batavia it was as rare to see a Chinaman idle as it was to see a Dutchman or Indian at work.

By the 11th of November the ship's hull was thoroughly put into repair; but rigging, getting water and various stores on board, took up the time until the 24th of December, when Cook took leave of the governor and some of the chief people of the settlement, who had shown him much attention during his stay. On the 26th, under a salute of fourteen guns from the garrison, he weighed anchor, and sailed out of Batavia Roads, leaving seven of his company behind, in their graves.

The course was now homeward, across the stormy, vexed Indian Ocean, and round the Cape of Good Hope. But the invalids on board soon became worse, so that on the 5th of January, 1771, they touched at Prince's Island, a small well-wooded island at the western mouth of the Straits of Sunda, to get fresh provisions for them, as well as wood and water, which were wanted on board. Turtle, deer—so small that one on which they dined weighed only forty pounds—fowl, fish, fruit, and vegetables, were had here in plenty, and the natives traded pretty honestly, with this slight exception, that they asked a great deal more for their goods than they meant to take. Well laden with these good things, which were, indeed, life to the sickly crew, the "Endeavour" sailed again on the 15th, direct for the Cape. But that was a dreary run; for the sickness on board, despite the fresh food, increased to such an extent that, in the course of six weeks, twenty-seven men were laid in their last resting-place—the depths of the mighty ocean.

BOOBIES.

THE CAPE.

The run from Batavia to the Cape did not furnish much that is interesting. A few days after leaving Java Head those strange birds called boobies were seen about the ship. The booby is a large bird, about the size of a goose, brown on the back, and white on the under part of the body, and it has its name from the extreme stupidity with which it allows itself to be taken with the hand, or knocked down with a stick, without making the slightest attempt to get away. It roosts at night on some desolate island or shore in southern latitudes, so that when seen flying about a ship, or settling on the shrouds, it is always supposed that land is not far off. Off Madagascar great numbers of albatrosses were met with. Stewed albatross they had already found to be a very satisfactory dish.

On, on, through the solitary waters, until the high, naked mountains of the Cape—stern and desolate-looking after the rich scenery that had so long met their eyes—came in sight; and on the 15th March the "Endeavour" cast anchor in its fine and safe bay. The colony at that time belonged to the Dutch, who were the first to settle at the Cape. We English made it our own in 1806.

The sick on board were Cook's first care, and he had the comfort of soon getting them lodged on shore, the governor promising him every care and attention.

The country about the Cape was then much more desert-like than it is now. Its climate, of course, has not changed, though climates do change very much with cultivation of the soil, and planting. Draining can convert an unhealthy swamp into wholesome, productive country; and trees influence the fall of rain, not only as to the quantity of it, but the manner in which it comes down: both of which are of great importance, not only to agriculture, but to the health of man. The Cape country has still its torrent of rain at one season, and its sandy deserts at another. The settlers there at the time of Cook's visit were "few and far between." A farmer who came to Cape Town from his home, fifteen days' journey off, bringing his little children with him, was asked why he had not left them with his nearest neighbour, rather than drag the little things all that dreary way. "Neighbour!" said he; "why, my nearest neighbour is five days' journey off."

Cape Town, which was entirely built by the Dutch, at this time contained one thousand brick houses, thatched, for no other roofing could have withstood the violence of the north-east wind to which it is exposed. The town had been planned after the Dutch fashion: broad streets, cutting straight across each other, with a canal, whose banks were planted with oaks, running through the principal one.

The Dutch were always excellent farmers and gardeners, so that there was good beef, mutton, and butter to be had, as well as European wheat, barley, vegetables and various kinds of fruit.

Of the natives, none were seen, excepting those employed as servants by the Cape farmers. These were of the middle height, slender, rather thin, but very strong and active. Fat people, indeed, are seldom strong: it is your wiry fellows that do the work. Their skins were dark, as well as dirty; the hair black, hanging in closely-twisted curls; their eyes dull, with no meaning in them. The dress was a sheepskin thrown over the shoulders; but, of course, they had their bits of finery, in the shape of bead necklaces and bracelets, worn by men and women alike, who also rubbed themselves all over with grease; fresh butter was the modish wear: it was made by shaking milk in a bag made of hide.

Having had what refreshment was required at the Cape, the ship stood out of the bay on the morning of April the 14th. Want of wind detained her for several days off a small island, also belonging to the Dutch, and used by them as a place of confinement for such of their worst criminals as were not quite bad enough to be put to death. On attempting to land here for some cabbages, they were warned off; and as the warning was backed by a little troop of six musketeers, it was thought proper to obey it. It was well for the guard of these criminals to be alert, for a Danish vessel, short-handed by the sickness of her crew, had once sent a boat on shore here, and, by force, carried off as many of the convicts as she required to man the vessel home. Rather high-handed, that!

St. Helena, now a regular calling-place for vessels crossing the Atlantic—indeed, a sort of ocean post-office —was next touched at, and a few days were spent there. The island is a huge rock, rising from the ocean so steeply that, at a very short distance from the shore, the sounding-line finds no bottom.

The remainder of the voyage home was done in safety, though the rigging and sails were so thoroughly worn out, that something or other was always giving way. Patching and mending, however, carried them through; and on the 12th of May, 1771, the "Endeavour" came to anchor in the Downs, after having sailed round the world from east to west, and been absent from England nearly three years.

CHAPTER VII.

SECOND VOYAGE ROUND THE WORLD, IN 1772, 1773, 1774, AND 1775.—OBJECTS OF THE VOYAGE.—IN THE ICE.—CROSS THE ANTARCTIC CIRCLE.—LOSE SIGHT OF THE "ADVENTURE."— RUN TO NEW ZEALAND.—DOINGS THERE.

COOK was now at home again, but not to rest. Men like him are too valuable to the world to be left in lazy do-nothingness. And to such as he, an idle life would be the most intolerable fate to which they could be doomed. Wearing out, not rusting out, must be their lot—the most respectable lot that can fall to any one.

Cook had not been on shore many months before it was proposed to him to go out again, to search more closely for that unknown southern continent of which people had been dreaming for nearly two centuries, and still dreamed; as well as to complete his exploration of the Southern Ocean. What he had already done, had proved that this continent was not situated exactly where it had been supposed to be; still, it might exist somewhere further south than his first voyage round the world had carried him.

The present expedition was to be on a larger scale than

the former one; two vessels were to be sent, instead of one only. They were both small, like the "Endeavour," who had done her work so well, that it was thought her build could not be improved upon. The "Resolution," of 462 tons burden, was placed under Cook's own command: he had, for his services, just been promoted to the rank of commander in the Navy, usually called captain; and the "Adventure," of 336 tons, was to be commanded by Lieutenant Furneaux, who had been out with Captain Wallis, when he sailed in those seas. The crew of the former, all hands included, numbered 112 souls; that of the latter, 81. Several of his officers had been with Cook on his former voyage, so that he knew the stuff they were made of; the others were also picked men.

The stores of both ships were abundant—provisions for two years and a-half for each; and they were well-chosen for preserving the health of those on board. Among them were malt, which was to be steeped as if for brewing, and the liquor, called wort, given to such as showed any symptoms of scurvy; sour-krout, made by cutting cabbage small, with salt, juniper berries, and aniseed, the mess (disagreeable enough, one thinks, though it was very wholesome) being then fermented, and afterwards pressed closely down in casks. Of this, which would keep good for a long time, one pound per man was given twice a-week, or oftener if needful, when fairly out at sea. Then there was cabbage salted down plain; portable soup, to be boiled with peas, and with vegetables, when they could be had; juice of lemons and of oranges; sugar; wheat, for occasional use in place of oatmeal; saloop; marmalade made of carrot; beer and wort boiled down to a syrup: in short, everything that was either known or supposed to be good for keeping off the dreaded sea-scurvy.

A draughtsman, to sketch the scenery and the people that came under their notice; two naturalists, to examine and describe the beasts, birds, fishes, and plants of the unknown regions to which they were sailing; and two astronomers, were added to the complement of men on board. The latter were well provided with the various delicate instruments required for their duties, which did not alone consist in looking after the sun, the moon, and the stars, in their places high up in the heavens, but in using these to draw out rules for the navigation, not only of the unknown seas to which they were proceeding, but of all waters that should be dashed aside by the bows and cut by the keel of a ship.

Cook's appointment to the "Resolution" was dated the 18th of November, 1771, but it was not until the 22nd of June, 1772, that he sailed from Sheerness, joining the "Adventure" at Plymouth on the 3rd of July. His instructions were delivered to him here. They were, that he should seek this unknown continent, by sailing round the world as near the South Pole as possible; now going east, now west, as circumstances might lead him, so as effectually to sweep the seas, and if there were no continent, to make out such islands as might lie in them; landing where possible, to study their inhabitants and gain all such knowledge either of land or sea as would be useful to navigation or to trade, or in simply enlarging our acquaintance with the surface of the globe. This was something like a roving commission; and, of all men, Cook was the man for it.

The ships left Plymouth on the 13th of July, reaching Madeira, their first halting place, where they were to take in wine, on the 29th. Thence direct to the Cape, calling at St. Jago, one of the Cape de Verde Islands, for water; the fort here, on receiving from Cook a salute of eleven guns, had the incivility to return it with only nine,—simply cheating him out of two guns. This was a grave breach of naval etiquette, but, as an excuse was offered next day, it was forgiven. Fresh provisions were also had here, which were more to the purpose than any amount of salutes; but the heavy rains that fell for several days whilst they were filling the water-casks, much endangered the health of the crew. Airing and drying the ship between decks, and making the people wash and dry their clothes, were the measures resorted to as the best to avoid injury from this hot, damp weather.

At two in the afternoon of the 29th of October, the shadowy, cloud-shrouded form of the vast Table Mountain rose up in the distance, and our voyagers hoped to cast anchor at its feet before nightfall. The name of this mountain has been given to it on account of its very singular appearance, as though its upper part had been cut off midway; and when the clouds descend upon its summit, that is called "laying the table-cloth." They were disappointed in their hope of anchoring, having to stand off and on the night through. Soon after eight in the evening, the sea all around seemed suddenly on fire with that phosphorescent light, the cause of which had so much puzzled all

TABLE MOUNTAIN.

the wise heads that had seen it: some supposing that it was produced by a peculiar kind of insect, others denying this. To make sure, Cook had a quantity of the shining, flashing water drawn up at the ship's side, and then it was proved, beyond doubt, that insects were the cause of this singular appearance: small, round, transparent creatures, the size of a pin-head. *What* their light is, is another thing; most likely it is similar to that of the glow-worm, which it resembles. On a dark night, this appearance of the water is exceedingly beautiful—as though the sea were all alight with a pale, changing, quivering flame. The moist sea-sand also partakes of it.

On mooring in Table Bay, next morning, Cook got his eleven guns duly in return to his own salute. The Dutchmen knew what was proper, and they did it. He also got fresh meat, and his ship, which was a little the worse for wear with the run from Plymouth, was fresh painted and caulked. Caulking is cramming the seams of a ship's deck or sides with oakum, to make them water-tight: it is hammered in with an iron tool and a mallet. All this took time, longer than he liked, so that it was the 22nd of November before he weighed and bore away south: not to the sunny south, but the south of antarctic frost and cold, which is considered to be greater than that of the opposite Pole. Extra warm clothing was now served out, and on the 10th December they came in sight of their first island of ice. There were plenty more where that came from, for it was speedily found that amid snow, sleet, and haze, they were steering right for another iceberg, half-a-mile or so in extent, standing fifty feet out of the water, with sides like a wall, against which the breaking waves dashed high in a cloud of foam. It was cautious sailing after this narrow escape—with close reefed topsails, and the lead kept continually going, to measure what depth of water they had,—feeling their way, as one might call it, among these dangerous neighbours, any one of which would have been enough to smash them to pieces, had the ship been driven against it.

Ice, ice, ice: though it was not winter in this region, but summer,—to wit, December, our mid-winter in northern latitudes. But though ice was dangerous, either in hillocks to go crash against, or in large flat fields to be frozen up in for the winter (perhaps cracked, like a walnut, between two meeting together), or to be more quietly stuck fast, and floated off, nobody knows where, yet it had also its uses to our navigators; for ice will thaw, and from time to time a good haul of it was made, broken up with pickaxes to get it aboard, and afterwards melted in the coppers, furnishing them with a good supply of fresh, sweet water; for what little salt water hung about it soon drained off. It was a slow process to fill the water-casks in this manner, but not slower than by the ordinary methods. In five or six hours as much ice was got as yielded fifteen tons of water. In a tropical sea, under such circumstances, they might have perished with thirst. Meanwhile, the snow and sleet froze on the rigging as it fell, making ropes and blocks so slippery as to render the handling of them not a little difficult.

By the 17th of January, 1773, the Antarctic Circle had been crossed, and then it was, "No road this way!" Ice here, ice there; and, more especially, a solid bar of ice ahead of them in their southern course—a bar that there was no getting round nor breaking through—put a complete stop to further progress in that direction. Winter, too, was coming on, so the gallant commander and his noble ship had just to put about, and go back again in search of more open seas.

A dark-brown bird seen at this time, about the size of a large crow, and of a kind not usually met with far from shore, would have led to the idea of land not being far off, perhaps that very continent they were so anxiously in search of. But birds, as well as ships, may travel far on an ice-island, and so the solitary Port Egmont hen went for nothing, so far as indicating land was concerned.

On the northward course frequent communication was had with their companion, the "Adventure," who, on the morning of February the 7th, had been signalled to keep about four miles on the starboard—that is, right-hand—of the "Resolution." The weather being hazy, next day guns were fired by the "Resolution" every hour until noon. Signal was then made for the "Adventure" to tack; but as no answering signals had been received for some time, it was feared the two had parted company. This, indeed, proved to be the fact; nor did they meet again until the 18th of May, when the "Resolution," sailing into Queen Charlotte's Sound, New Zealand, found her consort comfortably at anchor there, where she had been for six weeks. Of course such a chance as parting company had been foreseen by Captain Cook, who had given Furneaux directions as to what he should do in that case.

Whilst in this cold region, the northern lights, as we Northerns call them, were seen on the 16th of February:

somewhat to Cook's surprise, who thought they were only seen in the north. There, however, they were, southern lights, or streamers, as well as northern ones.

On the 21st, another strange sight met their eyes, for, on steering towards a large ice-island, half-a-mile round, and three or four hundred feet above the water, it canted, and turned over in the water almost upside down. What a commotion such a mass must have made, in the course of its revolution! These numerous ice-islands floating about, grand and fantastic, together with the large fragments that from time to time broke off them, forming still more dangerous blocks, as being less easily seen and guarded against than their parent masses, decided Cook against a second crossing of the Antarctic Circle, which he had desired; so, on the 17th of March, having well assured himself that no southern continent was to be found where he was seeking it, he made up his mind to steer direct for New Zealand, both to refresh his people and to look for Furneaux. He hoped to touch at Van Diemen's Land on the way, in order to make out whether it was a separate island or a part of New Holland; but the wind being against him, he was compelled to run direct for New Zealand, entering Dusky Bay, on the south of what is now called the Middle Island, or New Munster, on the 26th of March, after having been nearly four months at sea, without sight of land, and having in that time sailed over some fourteen thousand miles of an ocean, the greater portion of which had been unvisited by man before.

Thanks to his never-tiring care of his crew, Cook brought them all, save one man, in tolerable health and strength into this much-needed resting-place of Dusky Bay; and having killed a seal, which made them a good dinner, they settled down snugly in their new quarters. Seals were by no means bad meat, reminding the eater, now of pork, now of beefsteak. What could hungry Englishmen desire more?

Pickersgill Harbour, as it was named, after one of Cook's lieutenants, who was fortunate enough to find it out, was one of the most charming places in the world to moor the "Resolution" in. It fitted the ship like a glove. Wood was close at hand, for the ship's yards poked their way in and out among the branches of the trees growing by its side; and a stream of water wimpled along almost under her very stern; whilst fish and wild-fowl appeared to be plentiful in sea and on land around them. To work at once! Up with the tents, for the scientific gentlemen to peer at the stars and map their wanderings, and for the unscientific folk to mend sails, hoop casks, and do other mean work! Hammer and anvil soon made the woods ring, as the armourer and his mate wrought at their forge; and the busy family was completed by wood-cutters, watering-parties, brewers of spruce-beer from the overhanging trees, and the various other busy workers, gentle and simple, engaged on this welcome bit of land life, after the cold perils of the Southern Ocean.

A few sheep and goats that were left on board were brought ashore to have their share of the change; but the poor beasts had got a touch of sea-scurvy, and their teeth were so loosened by it that they in vain tried to crop the herbage, such as it was, or even the tender-leaved plants around.

This southern portion of the Middle Island of New Zealand—or, as Cook, only knowing two islands, would have called it, the Southern Island—had never before been visited by Europeans; so that his stay here was breaking fresh ground, as well as refreshing his wearied, weather-beaten people.

Some of the natives were presently seen about, but they were very shy; and though trinkets of various kinds were placed in the canoe which they left hauled up on the beach, the owners did not return to get them.

A shooting party or two that went out had varying luck. One brought home a welcome supply of wild-fowl; the other, going out in more formal fashion, with a dog which they had picked up at the Cape, returned ignominiously, with nearly empty bags, and *minus* their dog, which had bolted into the woods when the first shot was fired, and whence they had not been able to persuade the return of the interesting creature. On one particular day so many ducks were secured for the spit by the captain and his companions, on the north side of the bay, that the site of their capture was distinguished as Duck Cove. On returning from this onslaught, three natives, a man and two women, all armed, the man with a club, the women with spears, were met with. They at first seemed frightened, but friendly gestures at last reassured them, and after a cheerful half-hour's chat, not much understood on either side, they went off pleasantly enough. Other interviews followed; but on the 9th of April, when their English visitors went to meet them, no notice was taken of the shouting and hallooing with which they announced their coming. The cause of this was soon seen: their new friends were all as busy as

MAN AND WOMAN. NEW ZEALAND.

possible in their huts, preparing for a full-dress reception of their distinguished guests. The finishing touches were completed at last, and there they stood in all their holiday clothing—with their hair oiled, and trimmed with feathers stuck upright or in wreaths round their heads, and bunches of white feathers worn as earrings. They were very courteous, as people who know they are thoroughly well-dressed are apt to be. The chief blandly accepted a cloak which he had begged on a former occasion; it was made of red baize, and won his heart so completely, that in return he gave Captain Cook the patoo-patoo from his own girdle. An European monarch, less than a century ago, would have presented his own snuff-box to one whom he desired to honour.

Duck-shooting, fishing, two or three seals shot—for food, for oil, and their skins for rigging—and some interviews with the natives, filled up the time of those who were not at work upon the ship, or attending to the wants of her crew, for several more days. A chief who, with his daughter, came on board on the 18th, went through a singular little ceremony before setting foot on board the vessel, beating her side with a small green branch, whilst he repeated a prayer or speech, and afterwards throwing the branch into what are called the main chains. It was understood as a peace-making ceremony. This chief made his English acquaintances very profitable ones, obtaining from them in the course of his visits nine or ten hatchets, plenty of spike nails, and other articles. The hatchets and nails he always stuck to; other matters were laid down as they were given to him, and often left behind. Replete with these good things, of which he now had more than any other man in the country, he at length went his way and they saw him no more. It is said that people never think they have enough: they always want a little more than they have got. Our New Zealander was an exception to this rule.

It has been mentioned that it was part of Cook's plan to stock the various islands he visited with useful animals and vegetables. A quiet spot, far enough from the haunts of the islanders to be secure from their disturbance, was now chosen for leaving the five geese which he had brought from the Cape; and in honour of them the place where they were turned out was named Goose Cove. It was needful to choose an unvisited bit of country for these most useful "settlers"—beasts or birds, as might be—in order that they might not be killed and eaten the moment the donor's back was turned, but, instead of that, might have time to increase until the island should become stocked with them. The benevolence of such conduct is admirable; or, rather, it should be said, beneficence—because benevolent only means *wishing* good, which a man may do in his easy chair, with his heels on the fender; beneficence means *doing* good, and that requires labour and self-sacrifice. Several kinds of garden seeds were also sown here, for the benefit of the islanders: the ground being first prepared by burning the shrubs to dry it, and digging it well over; for there is great virtue in thoroughly exposing soil to the air.

The soil in this neighbourhood appeared to be good—a deep black mould—and yet there was very little herbage, the only eatable plants found being a few watercresses and a little celery, nor were there fruit trees of any value. Indeed, in recent times, it has been doubted whether the soil of New Zealand is really a good one; some say it is wanting in those elements of a soil that are requisite for life-sustaining crops. Fish was abundant in the bay, and good; seals numerous; five kinds of ducks were met with, some of beautiful plumage, as well as other birds; one lovely little creature called a fantail, whose body was scarcely larger than a good filbert, whilst its tail was like that of a peacock on a small scale, spreading like a fan, with beautifully-coloured feathers four or five inches long. The country was mountainous, and well wooded towards the coast. The people were evidently of the same race as those inhabiting the northern portion of New Zealand, formerly visited by Captain Cook.

Dusky Bay, especially that nice little Pickersgill Harbour, was altogether a desirable resting place, spite of its being so rainy, and wretchedly infested by stinging sand-flies. But the rain did nobody any harm; and ship and crew being alike made over again by their stay here, it was time to be gone. This, however, was sooner said than done; calms detaining the "Resolution" for four days after she first attempted to leave the bay. A favourable wind at last sprang up, and on the 11th May, leaving that part of the coast, they bore away towards their old quarters in Queen Charlotte's Sound, where they expected to find the "Adventure."

Nothing worthy of notice occurred during the sail thither until the 17th of May when, the wind suddenly falling, with a dark, cloudy sky, six waterspouts were seen forming.

First, the surface of the water, for a space of 150 feet or so, foamed, and splashed, and churned, rising as it whirled, until it met a depending portion of the cloud, which looked like a descending column of water. When united, the column gradually increased in bulk for a time, then gradually diminished, until it parted towards its base, the upper part appearing to be drawn up into the clouds again, whilst the sea resumed its former appearance. It was thought that a bird was seen whirled round in one of these spouts, which, first perceived two or three miles off, moved onwards to within fifty yards of the ship's stern, but without doing any damage. Their breaking close to a ship sometimes gives it a very inconvenient kind of shower-bath. Next day the Sound was in sight, and, to their great joy, they discovered their missing companion the "Adventure," which had been lying there six weeks, and whose boats were now sent out to tow the "Resolution" into the Sound. Captain Furneaux had lost sight of the "Resolution" in a fog, which had also deceived him as to the direction of Cook's signal guns; so, after cruising about for three days, hope of rejoining her was given up, and they forthwith took their course to Queen Charlotte's Sound for the winter, having at the time only one quart of water per day for each man. Van Diemen's Land was taken by them on their way, and, going on shore, five days were spent there in getting wood and water, and making the "Adventure" a little more ship-shape than her beating about in high latitudes had left her. The country seemed a pleasant one, evergreen trees clothing the sides of the hill, the soil rich, though scanty. Of inhabitants they saw none. Two

rather severe gales had been encountered by them on their voyage, which was at last safely ended in the Sound. The "Adventure's" coasting Van Diemen's Land had pretty well made out what Cook had wished to ascertain, namely, that it and New Holland were two islands, and not one, as had been supposed.

Whilst in the Sound they had received visits from the natives, some of whom asked about Tupia, and when told he was dead, seemed much grieved, inquiring further whether the English had killed him. These people had brought plenty of fresh food, and made themselves very friendly.

CHAPTER VIII.

QUEEN CHARLOTTE'S SOUND.—THE SOCIETY ISLANDS AGAIN.

ON the morning after his arrival in Queen Charlotte's Sound, Captain Cook went out to look for vegetables, and fortunately came back with his boat laden with scurvy-grass, celery, and other plants of the kind, which he ordered to be boiled with wheat and peas and portable soup, for the crews of both vessels, in order to remove the effects of their long-continued salt meat diet. The men did not at first like such wholesome additions to their fare as their commander was from time to time anxious to provide for them; nor did the officers: it was something new, and, therefore, must certainly be bad; and, finally, neither officers nor men would eat the stuff. If they had ventured to speak their minds about it, no doubt it would have been to the effect that the captain might eat it himself! But Cook was not a man to be foiled in what he knew to be right: he would not have been fit for his post if he had been. He calmly persevered in his wise measures, without noticing the opposition with which he was met. At length his people condescended to taste what they scorned; found it not so bad as they had fancied; and, lastly, experiencing the beneficial effect of it, soon became quite as eager as the commander himself, wherever they touched, to go ashore and hunt for vegetables.

As Cook did not intend to stay in the Sound any longer than he could help, he was busy enough during his brief sojourn there. A couple of sheep, that he had brought with him from the Cape, were at once sent on shore, for the purpose of stocking the country with those valuable animals—valuable alike for their meat and for their wool. But, alas! in a day or two they were found dead—poisoned, it was supposed, by something they had cropped among the grass. So, adieu to broadcloth and blankets; adieu to mutton—so far as they were concerned. Captain Furneaux had, on his arrival, planted some garden seeds and roots, which were doing well; and Cook set his people to work to plant more seeds, as well as roots, such as turnips, carrots, and parsnips. These seemed to be valued; one of the natives was so pleased with the potatoes that had been set by the master of the "Adventure," that he immediately began to hoe them in a proper manner. The other roots were then shown to him, and it was thought that the people might learn to cultivate them. Some goats and pigs were also put on shore, in hope that they would do better than the unfortunate sheep. The natives about were friendly, paying visits to the ship, and bringing fish and other articles for sale. On one of these visits, a man begged a white shirt for his son, a lad of nine or ten years old; and when it was given him, the little fellow went about in it, all over the ship, showing his finery to everybody that he met. But, as ill luck would have it, while he was going hither and thither in all his glory, an old goat that was on deck gave him such a prod with its horns as sent him, shirt and all, sprawling on his back. Boy was none the worse for his tumble, when he had picked himself up ; not so shirt, which was so dirtied in the scuffle that its owner was almost inconsolable, complaining bitterly of the bad manners of the " great dog," as he called it, until a good-natured seaman washed and dried his much-prized garment for him, and so restored him to peace of mind. Some of the people seen here inquired about Tupia, and seemed much concerned on finding that he was dead. It seemed strange that, on anchoring in this Sound, there was not among the natives a single face that Cook knew. He could only suppose that those who dwelt here at the time of his former visit had either been driven out, or changed their quarters of their own free will. Many empty huts were seen in the neighbourhood. As for their inquiry about Tupia, that was easily accounted for. Tupia, from his connection with the foreigners, had become a world's wonder all over New Zealand, so that the fame of him would spread even among those who had never seen him.

Both ships being now ready for sea, they sailed once more in company on the 7th of June, to continue that exploration of the southern seas which was Cook's great object. Tahiti was to be his first land, which was made at four o'clock in the morning of the 26th of August. It was rather bad sailing, a day or two previously, among a number of low, sunken, "half-drowned" isles, which very properly received the name of Dangerous Archipelago.

Both ships had a narrow escape of being wrecked in endeavouring to get into Oaiti-piha Bay, near the south-eastern end of the island, a number of natives, both on board and hanging about, looking on with the most placid indifference whilst the two were thus endangered. Fortunately, they escaped with the loss of some of their anchors and hawsers.

It was found that many of their old friends in this part of Tahiti were dead, slain in battle; and some of their new ones proved not a little troublesome. Pilfering went on gaily on board ship, and at length Cook got so tired of it, that he ordered the whole lot of them to be turned out. He was so provoked at one fellow, that he could not help firing a couple of muskets over his head, by way of speeding his flight, which frightened the retreating thief so, that he at once bounced out of his canoe into the water. The captain also confiscated a couple of their canoes, as punishment for some stone-throwing at his people. There was a little boy in one, who was terribly frightened on finding himself in strange hands, but the kindly captain set him up with a gift of beads, and then put him on shore again. After this, both parties soon forgave each other, and all was right again, until a musket was stolen from the guard on shore. This was a serious offence; but some natives, in their friendliness, turned thief-catchers, knocked the culprit down, took the musket from him, and restored it to the owners.

One of the chiefs played the captain a very neat trick here. He came on board, politely offering a present of fruit and cocoa-nuts; but when the latter were opened, they were found to be what had already been tapped by the crew, for their milk, and then thrown over the ship's side. The donor was not at all put out by the discovery of his cheat; he opened two or three himself, as if to make sure that it was really so, and then, as coolly as though he had done nothing amiss, returned to the shore, whence he sent off a supply of plantains and bananas.

Finding that hogs were very scarce—for the stock of food-animals seemed to be much lessened since his former visit—Captain Cook decided on going to another part of the island, Matavai Bay, to procure them. Meanwhile, the leading chief of the district where he then was, made his appearance with a numerous retinue, and received the captain (who had seen him when a boy, in 1769) in something of state. The great man was seated on a stool in the open air, and having made his visitor sit down upon it by his side, the other officers being seated on the ground, proceeded to inquire about several of those who had been with the captain on his former visit. He was very civil, keeping Captain Cook close to him all the morning, and making him sit upon his own stool, which was carried from place to place by one of his servants. Of course, he got plenty of presents in return: medals—a number of which, with the head of George III. on one side and two ships on the other, had been struck by the Admiralty at home on purpose for such occasions—nails, knives, looking-glasses, a shirt, and other articles. These were acknowledged by the gift of a hog to each of the commanders. Others were got by trading, so that the crews had that day a hearty dinner of fresh pork.

MATAVIA BAY, TAHITI.

At their old quarters in Matavai Bay they were recognised by many of their old acquaintances, and were well received by the king, Otoo, a fine, well-made man of about thirty years of age, but so afraid of the guns that it was with no small difficulty that he was persuaded to come on board the "Resolution." He did get up his courage at last, and came with an imposing train, on the morning of the 27th of August, having also his sister and younger brother with him. Presents were made to all of them in return for those sent by the king, and after breakfast the captain took the whole family home in his boat. On landing, an old woman, mother of Tootahah, one of Cook's earliest friends on his first landing in Tahiti, seized both the captain's hands, and, weeping, exclaimed, in her own tongue, "Tootahah, your friend, is dead!" This was done with so much warmth of feeling that Cook, man as he was, was affected almost to tears. The king at once led her away; but the captain contrived to see the poor old creature again, when he gave her an axe and other presents. She must have been a loving mother, uncivilised as she was, for she could never afterwards see the white friend of her dead son without weeping. Captain Furneaux gave the king a couple of goats, in the hope that they might, in time, stock his territory with those useful beasts, which, both for their meat and their hair, may be called the sheep of those countries where sheep are either unknown or rare.

Otoo, having got over his terror of the guns, came on board a second time, again bringing his sister with him; when, in addition to gifts bestowed upon him, Captain

Cook did his best to dress the lady up, with such materials as he had. It is to be feared he made a sad "guy" of the poor unconscious princess, for gentlemen do not usually excel in millinery; but the critics would be limited to his own people, and they would have their laugh out quietly on board. Among the presents to the king was a sword, which frightened him nearly as much as the guns had done. He endured it, girded to his waist, for a while, but soon unbuckled it and sent it out of his sight. A rather unpleasant matter happened after this: some of the crew conducted themselves so badly on shore that both Otoo and many of his scared subjects fled in the night to the interior of the island; and when, at length, he was hunted up—for Cook wanted to take leave of him—he complained, justly, of the disturbance that had been made. As this was to be the last interview, three sheep that he had before seen, coveted, and begged for—nothing was lost here for want of asking for—were given to him; and in the fulness of his royal heart he returned the valued present with three hogs: one for Captain Cook, another for Captain Furneaux, and the third for Mr. Foster, the naturalist attached to the expedition. Presently afterwards one of his subjects was seen speaking warmly to him: what he said could not be clearly made out, but it was evidently about pigs; and as the man then took one of them away with him, they could only suppose he was scolding his master for overliberality. It turned out quite the contrary: he had taken away the smallest of the pigs, to bring back a larger one in its place.

Poor old Oberea was seen by Mr. Pickersgill the day

BAY OF HUAHEINE, SOCIETY ISLANDS.

before the vessels left, looking lower down in the world than ever.

During this second visit to Tahiti, Captain Cook clearly ascertained that it was a native custom to sacrifice human beings to their god.

Leaving the island on the 1st September, Huaheine was made the next day. The "Resolution" anchoring comfortably in twenty-four fathoms on the 3rd, the "Adventure," in attempting to do the same, got aground; happily, she was soon got off, none the worse for her mischance. Their reception here was a very gratifying one; abundant provisions were brought, and Cook's old acquaintance, Oree, with whom he had exchanged names in 1769, was, they were told, anxious to see his white friend again. But when great people meet, wearisome ceremonies must come between, which may make some of us thankful that we are not great people. When the captain went on shore to see the king, he was desired not to leave his boat, which was drawn up over against the chief's house, until five young plantain trees had been brought one by one to him. The first three trees were accompanied by three little pigs, whose ears were ornamented with fibres of cocoa-nut; a dog flanked the fourth. Each of these was understood to have some deep signification: Cook did not know what, possibly the natives did not either; but it was "correct," and so they did it. Lastly, the piece of pewter, with its inscription, and the other things given to Oree in 1769, were brought to the captain in the bag he had himself placed them in. There was no mistaking the friendly meaning of this. Then the visitors were bidden to hang up looking-glasses, nails, and trinkets of all sorts, on three young plantain trees, after the manner of Christmas trees; which done, the three were solemnly borne in their own hands through a lane of admiring natives, up to the chief himself, before whom, one by one, the trees were laid: one for God, another for the king, the third for friendship, as they were told. Ceremony was then at an end; and the old king, advancing to his friend, threw his arms around him, and literally wept upon his neck, like an eastern patriarch of Old Testament times. Cook respected this chief, who was worthy the regard of such a man as the captain. The old man did not limit his kindliness to weeping upon his friend's neck. He made it more substantial, for under his influence all that was wanted for the ships was readily got on the island; and to show his especial regard for the captain himself, he every day sent him an abundant supply of ready-dressed roots and vegetables. Deeds, not words! Those are the best, whether it be among heathen savages or civilised Christians.

The sterling character of this fine old man was still more strikingly displayed in a difficulty that arose afterwards. First, a foolish fellow of a chief made himself as disagreeable as he possibly could, by prancing about in his war-dress, with a club in each hand, evidently thirsting for mischief. Him Captain Cook quashed on the spot, treating the braggart as he deserved by taking his weapons from him, and breaking them before his face. But as the simpleton was a chief, it was thought that he might, in revenge, stir up strife in some shape or other; so a guard, hitherto unneeded for the trading party, was sent on shore. Next,

Mr. Sparrman, the botanist, thinking of nothing but his plants and tin cases, having gone out alone, was set upon, beaten with his own sword, stripped to his trousers, and then sent adrift. A friendly native bundled him up in a piece of cloth, and, thus made presentable, brought him to the place where trade between the English and the natives was being carried on : the latter starting off post haste at the first glimpse of the unfortunate Mr. Sparrman. Captain Cook could not pass over so gross an outrage as this. Beating the botanist, and reducing him to so very slender an amount of clothing—little as a native would have thought of the latter—was a very serious matter in the eyes of their foreign visitors. So a complaint was carried to Oree, who again " lifted up his voice and wept," with his chiefs, when he heard of the bad conduct of his subjects. He reproached his people bitterly for their misdoings and ingratitude to those who had, in so many ways, been their benefactors ; then, taking an account of all that Mr. Sparrman had been robbed of, he got up and coolly stepped into Cook's boat. A pretty howl was set up by the natives at this. They begged and prayed, they wept, and tried to pull him out. But Oree never minded them ; he felt his honour was at stake, and he was determined to find out the thieves, cost what it might. "Cook and I are friends," said he, in answer to their lamentations ; " why should I not go with him?" His sister, a high-minded woman, worthy of her brother, was the only one who did not oppose his going to hunt up the culprits. The boat then pulled off, and, after rowing some distance, the party landed, and went several miles into the interior, the king, as they proceeded, inquiring in all directions for trace of the thieves. The search was in vain; still, after he had treated his friends to cocoa-nuts, whilst they took a little rest, he would fain have had them go further with him in pursuit; but to this Captain Cook objected: it would have been taking more trouble than Mr. Sparrman's coat, waistcoat, and shirt were worth, even throwing in his sword also, which was the most valuable of his belongings. Besides, the general alarm raised had already stopped all trading with the natives, and, as he intended sailing next day, that was a serious inconvenience. So the baffled party returned, Oree still insisting on accompanying them to the ship, together with his sister, who had met them at their resting-place, and whose daughter, a girl of sixteen or so, cried, and tried hard to prevent her mother's running into danger—as she thought it. The two stayed to dinner on board, and Oree ate like a man with a good conscience—as he had a right to do—and a good appetite to boot. It was not etiquette for ladies of the Society Islands to eat in the presence of men; so the sister looked on, whilst her brother did full justice to English provisions and English cookery. When dinner was over, they were put ashore, none the worse, but the better, for the confidence they had placed in their white friend. Trading was immediately resumed, and everything was comfortable again.

The ships left next day, Captain Cook presenting the good old king—who would have had him stay to see the thieves punished (they were caught at last)—with another memento of this his second visit to Huaheine. It was a plate of copper, on which was engraved :—" Anchored here, His Britannic Majesty's Ships 'Resolution' and 'Adventure,'

September, 1773." This, together with some medals, was put in a bag, of which the chief promised to take care, and to show them to any vessels that might touch at Huaheine. He remained on board until the "Resolution" was near two miles from land, when, entering his canoe, he, with the help of one man who was with him, paddled himself to shore.

This Huaheine seemed a rich, productive island. Besides fowls and fruits, 300 hogs were had during the four days' stay here; nor, when the ships left, was there the slightest appearance of the stock getting low. Whilst at Huaheine, one of the natives of Ulietea, named Omai, had persuaded Captain Furneaux to take him to England with them. Cook was a little surprised at it, as he did not think this young man one of the best specimens of the people of the Society Islands. But Omai's conduct when in England, where he became an object of much attention and curiosity, was satisfactory, in the highest degree, to his benefactors. We shall meet him again before long.

At Ulietea also, to which they now sailed, our navigators were well treated by their old friends, who had not forgotten them. Canoes at once came off with hogs and fruit; and when, for want of room on board, purchase of some of these good things was refused, the generous islanders just handed them up on board, or tumbled them into the boats alongside, without staying to ask leave. Pleasant as everything seemed, our people, however, got a strange fright here one day. Finding that no canoes came off to the ship as usual, the two captains went ashore to see what was amiss. They scarcely found a soul there; a few of the people who ventured near them giving them to understand that several of their friends had been killed by the English, and others wounded, pointing out very particularly, at the same time, in what parts of the body the various balls had struck their victims. This was alarming, for as Captain Cook had sent some of his people to a neighbouring island to get vegetables, which were scarce here, he could only suppose they must have had a skirmish with the natives, and that they might consequently be now in danger. To make sure of this, he, with some difficulty, hunted up Oree, and then it all came out. Nobody was killed, nobody was wounded; but, seeing the boats go to Otaha (a neighbouring island), they had taken it into their heads that their crews had deserted; and, for fear they should themselves be punished as accomplices of the men, they had fled, chief and all: the ingenious story of the killed and wounded being invented to cover the real reason of their flight. It must be owned this was rather wholesale lying.

Two or three days before leaving Ulietea, Captain Cook invited himself to dine with the very friendly chief Oree. On arriving at his house, the floor was found thickly strewn with green leaves, as table-cloth and dishes in one; whilst hot bread-fruit and plantains were placed around, with cocoa-nuts for drink. The guests seated themselves round these leaves, and the meal was instantly served: first, one of the pigs—baked whole in the earth-oven—and then the other, coming souse over the captain's head on the leaves before him. Each man had his own knife in his hand, and, falling to at once, helped himself without ceremony, pieces of meat being occasionally handed to those sitting behind, for whom there was no space at table. The pork was exceedingly good, better than if roasted in our civilised way. Their host, unlike the rajah of Savu, having no fear of getting drunk before his eyes, took his glass of Madeira (brought by his foreign guests) as often as it came round ; and it seemed to agree with him. And so all ended pleasantly, the boat's crew, and some of the native people about, eating up the remains of the feast, so that nothing was left. The very crumbs were eagerly picked up by some of the common sort, who had only been spectators of the banquet.

Captain Cook took with him a young native lad when he sailed from Ulietea on the 17th of September. Several had offered themselves as his companions on board. He also took with him so many pigs, that there was scarcely room left to move about the decks, the two ships having between them three or four hundred squeaking, grunting beasts on board, whom it must have been a pleasure to eat up, if it were only to get rid of their noise.

CHAPTER IX.

FRIENDLY ISLANDS.—NEW ZEALAND AGAIN.—SAIL TO THE SOUTH.
—TURNED BACK BY ICE.—EASTER ISLAND.—THE MARQUESAS.
—A REVIEW OF WAR CANOES.—SOCIETY ISLANDS.

THE sailing course of the expedition was now westwards, slightly north, to avoid the tracks of former navigators. On the 23rd a small island was seen, to which the name of Hervey was given; and on the 2nd of October a landing was made in the island of Middleburgh, or Eahoowe, as the natives called it, one of the Friendly Islands, whose inhabitants seemed particularly kindly and confiding, bringing great baskets of cloths and matting, to exchange for nails; yet apparently not very anxious about getting anything in return, as some of them, who could not get near enough to the boats to trade, threw their bundles into them, over the heads of those who came between, and then at once went away. The party that went on shore was hospitably treated with bananas, cocoa-nuts, and other fruits, with ava to drink: Captain Cook being the only one amongst them who, having seen the mode of its preparation, ventured to taste it. Altogether it was a pleasant little visit to a pleasant little place.

In the evening sail was again made, for the neighbouring island of Amsterdam,—now known by its native name of Tongataboo,—a beautiful, well-cultivated spot, inhabited by a friendly, well-behaved people, with a decided tendency to thieving, from whom was obtained a liberal store of pigs and vegetable food. These were not only paid for in the current coin of those wild regions—goods of various kinds, among which old jackets and rags were not a little esteemed—but by more valuable gifts of garden seeds, which these clever folks well knew how to raise and cultivate. The king seemed a mere dolt—when a shirt was given him (which the donors had to put on him), he did not even take the trouble to raise his arms to help to get himself into it—but an intelligent chief, named Attago, who exchanged names with Captain Cook, according to the custom of the Society Islands, was very useful to the visitors. This man took the captain into one of their temples, or places of worship, a house about twenty feet long, and fourteen or sixteen broad, built, like the natives' own dwellings, with posts and rafters, thatched with palm leaves. The eaves reached to about three feet from the ground, that space being filled up with palm-leaf matting. The floor was of gravel, with the exception of an oblong square of blue pebbles in the centre, supposed to be an altar; though when Cook, thinking it safest to do so, placed some trifles upon it by way of offering, Attago coolly pocketed them himself. Two wooden images were inside this building, and on the captain's asking if they were gods, Attago tumbled them about so roughly as to show that *he*, at all events, did not think them so. The building was enclosed by an amazingly well-constructed wall of large blocks of a hard stone. Before entering the house, all sat down on the grass in front, whilst an old man, supposed to be a priest, made a speech or prayer, some ten minutes long. On returning from it they were taken to the dwelling of a chief, when again an old priest gave them a speech—not one word of which could they understand—directed first to the house of worship, then to the captain, and so on alternately, stopping at the end of every sentence addressed to the latter, until the guest so honoured nodded his satisfaction. Attago went on board with them to dinner; but ere they could sit down to it, another chief arrived, of so much superior rank that the poor man was obliged to go to the other end of the table, where, turning his back to the new comer, he picked a morsel furtively. When the old chief retired, Attago, now his own man again, sat down properly and finished his dinner, as well as a couple of glasses of wine. The old chief was owner of a fine large double canoe, as yet unlaunched, which he showed to the visitors with some pride. The canoes of these people were the best made that had been seen in the southern seas. Their cultivation of the land was also very superior to that of most of their neighbours in these wide seas—one fancies all the islands of the Pacific neighbours, spite of the thousands of miles between many of the groups. There scarcely seemed an inch of ground lost; even the fences were contrived to take up the smallest possible space, and sometimes were formed of useful plants.

The king and Attago, having both made presents to

Captain Cook, he, in return, gave them sundry articles, including a sheet and a checked shirt, both of which Attago dressed himself up in, one after the other, and then strutted about before his friends with much complacency. He was particularly anxious that when Cook came again he should bring him a naval uniform, like that worn by the captain.

The people of this island were light copper-coloured, with short, generally dark, hair, the men dying theirs white, blue, or red, sometimes all three colours on the same head. A copper-coloured Indian with a blue or tri-coloured "thatch" must have been a lively spectacle. Their dress was a piece of cloth or mat, reaching from the waist to below the knees. Their weapons were clubs, spears, with bows and arrows—these last not worth much; their instruments of music four-holed flutes, "pandean pipes," and long wooden drums, beaten on the side instead of the end. The women often sang to their guests, and their voices were sweet and tunable. Their mode of greeting their friends was by touching noses, as in New Zealand—not lips, as in Europe. Tattooing, and other ornaments, were used among them. Among their customs was, that every article given to a native was always first carried to the head, by way of thanks; even the little children were made to do this by their mothers. They had a strange practice in these islands, that of cutting off one or both little fingers : understood to be done in sacrifice to their gods, for the purpose of averting death from themselves or others. The name of Friendly Islands was given by Cook to this group, on account of the apparent good will of the natives.

On leaving Amsterdam the ships bore away towards the northern part of New Zealand, Captain Cook being anxious to give to the people of a rather less savage district there, the hogs and fowls, roots and seeds—enough, in time, to stock the island—which he had brought for the purpose, in hopes of naturalising them there. He did not land, but committed his treasures to a native, who came alongside in his canoe, and who had the appearance of a chief. The man faithfully promised not to kill the animals and poultry, but to leave them to multiply in the country; and then, carefully collecting them together, to be sure they were all there, he and his cargo took their departure. The people of this point, also, evidently remembered Cook's former visit, as their first words were, "We are afraid of the guns."

Stretching away now southwards, squalls and gales troubled them, and, in the midst of the bad weather, they again lost sight of the "Adventure"—this time for good, for they never met again, Captain Furneaux reaching England by himself on the 14th July, 1774.

Queen Charlotte's Sound, where Cook proposed calling for wood and water, before continuing his discoveries south and east, was reached in safety, on the 3rd November, 1773, though the "Resolution" had been much tossed about in the gales.

Cook was rather disappointed at the result of his efforts to benefit the natives of this place. The two goats he had left had been killed by a rascally chief, and the pigs had come to no good. The gardens they had been at the trouble to make were in better condition, for they had not been meddled with, and kindly mother Nature, according to her wont, had done her best for them. Most of the potatoes had been used. Not discouraged, however, by the mischances, more pigs and more poultry were left behind, some of them being landed, with a ten days' supply of food, in a spot where the natives would not find them for some time, just to give them a chance of establishing themselves in the island. Nay, such was this great man's thoughtful solicitude for the wild people of the Southern Ocean, that, in addition to the pigs, the sheep, the dogs, and the poultry that he put ashore from time to time, more than twenty cats were also, in the course of this cruise, bestowed upon his friends in the Society Islands. And it must not be forgotten that poor pussy is both a very useful and a highly respectable member of society, seeing that she not only fairly earns her own living by ridding your house of rats and mice, but does her own washing into the bargain!

Thieving seemed constitutional with the natives, as with most of those in these ocean islands. On this occasion, a chief made a great fuss about protecting his friends from the depredations of the common people; but, alas! the great man was himself caught picking Captain Cook's pocket of his handkerchief. When found out, he took it easily, laughed at the matter, and then coolly went on board to dine with the captain as if nothing had been amiss.

In course of their overhauling the ship, whilst in this Sound, the bread was found in so bad a state, that 4,292 pounds were totally unfit for use, and 3,000 more could only be eaten by very hungry people. The worst was picked out, and the remainder exposed to the air, and re-baked. In those days it was thought that ship-bread—that is, biscuit—kept better for being well exposed to the air: airing the bread-room being one of the regular duties on ship-board. It has now long been known that the best method of keeping it good is to have it made up air-tight. This looking over and throwing away a large quantity of bad bread had to be done over again at Tahiti a few months later.

The supply of fish, celery, and scurvy-grass was good here, and their own gardens furnished them with other vegetables; so that men and ship were well recruited when sail was made on the 25th. Before leaving, a memorandum, with directions for Captain Furneaux, if he should chance to touch there, was placed in a bottle, and buried at the root of a tree in their garden. In thus setting out alone to prosecute his arduous search of the southern seas, Cook was thankful that no one was discouraged by the loss of their companion. Solitary as they now were, both officers and men were as ready as himself to brave the dangers before them, and they cheerfully addressed themselves to their work.

Proceeding south, to look for that continent which seemed to fly from them as they pursued it, they soon got among ice again: large islands of it, to steer cautiously among; floating ice, to go crashing through; and immense fields, stretching far and wide, to bring them up with a full stop; whilst gales of wind, and storms of snow and sleet, freezing on the rigging as it fell, until the ropes could scarcely be worked, so added to the difficulties of navigation as, on the 23rd of December, to induce the captain to turn north again for a short time. But it was only "drawing back to leap further," as his next attack on the south carried him much deeper into the regions of ice, far within the antarctic circle ; and on the 30th of January, 1774, in latitude 71 deg. S., he found himself on the crumbling edge of a solid, illimitable field of ice, stretching far out of sight, both east and west. Ninety-seven ice-hills, some so lofty that they looked like a mountain chain whose peaks were lost in the clouds, were seen within this field ; others were outside it. It was impossible to cope with such an array, which in all likelihood extended to the Pole itself. Cook felt he had now pushed his way south to its utmost limits ; not one inch more could he make, and a retreat must therefore be beaten at once. His best plan, he considered, would be to proceed towards the tropic, winter there in case of need, enlarging or confirming his discoveries in that portion of the Southern Pacific, and, with returning summer, again pursue his researches in the extreme south, not only of the Pacific, but of the Atlantic Ocean. His course, zig-zagging about both oceans, as marked on the charts which were published on his return to England, looks not unlike an eccentric pattern for embroidery, or outlines of fortification. Officers and men entered heartily into his views, which were first to make for what is now known as the island of Juan Fernandez, on the coast of South America ; then south-west, to Easter Island ; and so on, westwards, among the numberless and little-known islands of the Southern Pacific, touching again at Tahiti, in hope of finding Furneaux there.

Captain Cook's own health had hitherto remained firm

amid all his anxieties and labours; but in the course of the run north it broke down, and he became so dangerously ill that all the skill of the surgeon on board, who was doctor and nurse in one, was taxed to save his life. During his recovery, with only salt meats on board, the difficulty was to find suitable diet for an invalid ; and as necessity has no law, Mr. Foster's dog was obliged to be turned into provision for the patient, who ate it, and soup made of it, apparently without distaste, and was certainly the better for this, which we should deem revolting food.

Easter Island came in sight on the 11th of March, but it was some time before a proper anchorage could be found. While they were seeking it, a canoe put off to them with a couple of men in it, who handed them some plantains in a very encouraging manner. Another of the natives was so exceedingly friendly, that he swam to the ship, and stayed on board two nights. All this was promising; but, when they went ashore, it was found there was not much to be got at Easter Island: no wood, no fish, no water worth having ; and though the people were peaceable and civil, they were, if possible, worse thieves than those already encountered. The very hats were scarcely safe on the heads of the visitors [it must be owned that in England we sometimes steal elderly people's gold spectacles off their noses!]; pockets seemed made only to be picked by the Easterlings, who, further, were so adroit at filching back again the various things they had sold, that the same article was sometimes bought by our people three or four times over, and they did not get it after all. These ingenious folk did not care whom they robbed ; one man coolly dug

STATUES—EASTER ISLAND.

up his neighbour's potatoes, in which he carried on a brisk trade with the ship until the owner appeared, full of righteous indignation, and put a stop to his dishonest marketing.

The island was chiefly remarkable for some immense statues, or rather busts, of stone, rudely sculptured, which had been noticed by earlier navigators. One of these measured fifteen feet in height, and six across the shoulders. What they were no one knew; some supposed them to be idols: Captain Cook thought they were merely to mark the burial places of the natives. A party from the ship, who took a walk into the country, were civilly marshalled along by a painted, tattooed old native, carrying a piece of white cloth on his spear, flag fashion; and in passing some huts were hospitably treated to roasted potatoes, sugar canes, and water to drink, which, though very bad, was most welcome to their thirsty throats. It was dealt out to them with scrupulous care that no one should get more than his neighbour. As for themselves, the custom of the place was to wash and drink in the same well, and at the same time.

Easter Island was left on the 15th, and favourable winds brought them in sight of the Marquesas, considerably north-west of it, on the 6th of April. Some of these islands had been discovered by the Spaniards, who gave them their names, in 1595; but Cook, or, rather, one of his officers, made out an additional one, which, in honour of the young man, received his own name, Hood Island. Anchor was cast in the Bay *Madre de Dios*, that is, Mother of God —changed by Cook to Resolution Bay—in the island of St. Christina. But their first dealings with the natives were marked by a melancholy occurrence, very rare under Cook's enlightened, firm command, one of them being shot dead, just after he had stolen an iron stanchion belonging to the gangway. The captain had noticed the great number of islanders on board, and their specially active thieving, so bade one of the officers look well after them, or something would be lost; then, finding the stanchion gone, he had given orders to fire, as usual, over their heads, but not to hurt any one. The noise was so great that he was not distinctly heard, so the thief was killed on the spot. The natives quickly disappeared for a while after this; but they did not seem to take it much to heart, as the next thing was a bold attempt to steal a buoy that marked the place where the anchor had been dropped, and it took two shots whizzing over the heads of these bold pilferers before they made up their minds to let it alone. Pigs, fruit, and water were had at this anchorage, though the trade in pigs was almost ruined by a young officer's paying for one with a large quantity of red feathers, which he had got at Tongataboo—red feathers being, of all things in the world most prized at the Marquesas; so that, when once seen, no other price in the shape of nails, beads, or the like, was looked at for a moment. This piece of mischief came of breaking, just for this occasion, Cook's rule, that one authorised person on board should manage all the traffic with the natives. The young gentleman had "put his foot in it," and, unfortunately, was not himself the sufferer. That is the worst of your insubordinate, wrong-headed people: they do the mischief, and others bear the brunt.

The inhabitants of these islands were the finest race yet

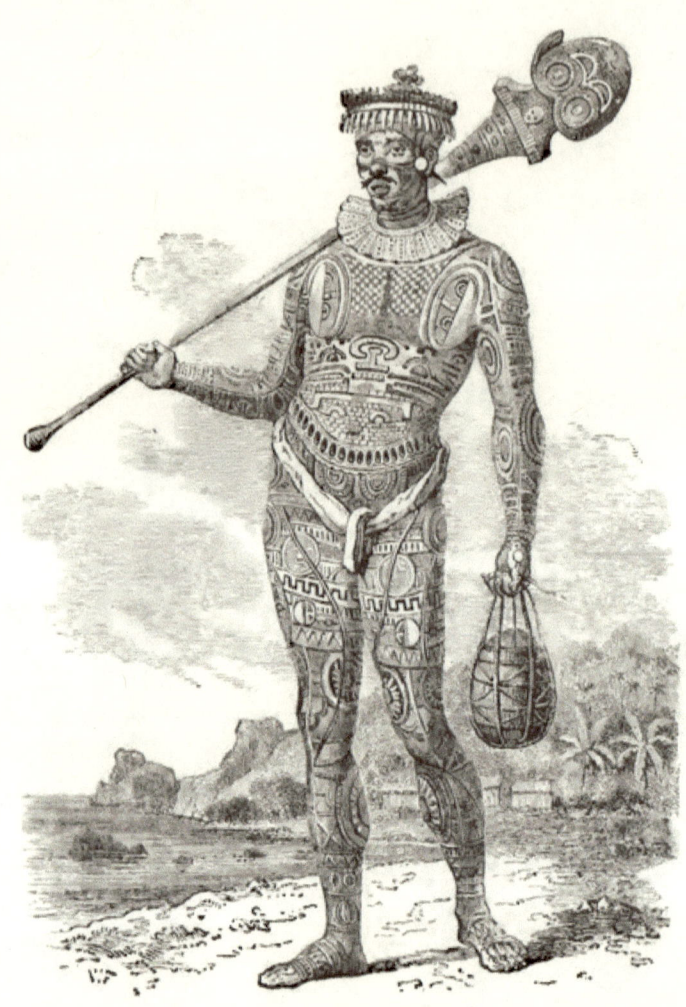

TATTOOED MARQUESIAN.

met with in the islands of the South Pacific. The men, who were from five feet ten to six feet high, were a good deal tattooed, which caused them to look darker than the women and young folks, who were content with very little of this peculiar decoration, and in consequence looked as fair as some Europeans. Their hair,—which, like that of Englishmen, was of various colours, red excepted,—was generally worn short, leaving a bunch at each side of the upper part of the head tied in a knot. The beard was sometimes long, hanging loose, or tied in two bunches under the chin; sometimes it was plaited. A sort of head-dress, made of fibres of cocoa-nut husk, and adorned with mother-of-pearl shell and small feathers standing on end, was much worn by them; and also a kind of broad frill of wood, on which small red peas were gummed, round the neck. Of clothing they had little; but ornaments were worn, as they seem to be everywhere all the world over, no matter how small the quantity of dress may be. Their houses were worse than those of their neighbours at Tahiti; nor were they as cleanly in their habits as the latter. Clubs and spears here were well made; they had also slings, but were bad "shots" with them.

Steering in a southerly direction after he left the Marquesas, Cook fell in with some more of those "half-drowned islands" as he called them, which seem to abound in that region of coral reefs; and as he had a mind to examine them, notwithstanding that the savages on their shores, armed with long spears, were seen moving along, as if on the look-out to give him an ugly greeting, he sent a couple of boats, with well-armed crews, ashore for this purpose. They were received peaceably by the stout, dark natives, though still in a manner that showed they were not wanted.

These half-drowned islands are formed by a circle of islets, joined to each other by a reef or wall of coral rock, outside of which the sea is unfathomable. Within it, the shallower water abounds with fish and turtle, serving as food for the inhabitants, and purchase-money for cloth from their more fortunate neighbours of the higher islands.

Matavai Bay, in Tahiti, was made on the 22nd of April, where their friend Otoo, the king, with his great people, seemed glad to see them, and their pleasure was greatly increased on finding that their friends had brought with them plenty of red parrot feathers from Amsterdam: these feathers being as highly valued here as in the Marquesas, so that as long as they lasted trading was easy. These red feathers were used in their religious rites, tied up in bunches of eight or ten and fastened to the end of a small cord, five or six inches long, made of the fibres of cocoa-nut, twisted until it was like wire: this was held between the finger and thumb whilst a prayer was recited. In case of need, two or three feathers sufficed. Those that are found on the head of the green paroquet were most esteemed; and such good judges of this particular commodity were the natives that it was in vain to attempt to pass off on them dyed feathers in place of the genuine ones. A longer stay than had been intended was made here; and this gave Cook additional opportunities of becoming acquainted with the ways and doings of the people.

A few days after their arrival, a review, on a large

I.

DOUBLE CANOE, SOCIETY ISLANDS.

scale, of what one might call the navy of the island, took place, to which the captain was invited, and almost dragged, with such hospitable warmth that he was in some danger of being torn to pieces. A hundred and sixty large war canoes, fully armed and equipped, with their fighting men in all their cumbrous war-dress aboard, were drawn up, like a fringe to the beach, heads to it, sterns to the sea; and with them were a hundred and seventy smaller double canoes, supposed to fill the place of our transports for the conveyance of stores, and the like: in all three hundred and thirty canoes, containing, it was calculated, between seven and eight thousand men. No trifling force this to launch against an offending neighbour, which was understood to be the present object of it: one of the adjacent isles having thrown off its allegiance to the Tahitian monarch. The war-dress consisted of breastplates, shields, so vast a quantity of cloth that the English spectators thought that the warriors must be somewhat fettered by it, turbans and helmets towering high and top-heavy above the heads of the wearers—perhaps to balance the unwieldiness of their "uniform." Their arms have been already described. The canoes were managed with great dexterity, the paddlers, well trained to the word of command, striking the water as one man, now on this side, now on that, now stopping, as signalled. When a landing was designed the canoes were formed in divisions of three, four, or more, close along side each other in a line as straight as an arrow, each division directed by a man bearing a wand, who was placed in the centre canoe. Then, on the signal being given, each squad of rowers dashed their paddles into the water, and, with might and main, rowed smartly to the shore, which was reached without the line being in the slightest degree broken, the warriors on the raised platforms in the canoes animating the rowers to their task. If it were wished to disperse on landing, each rower at once jumped out, and speedily, with the help of his comrades, dragged the canoes up on the beach, then walked off with his paddle, so that in a few minutes all trace of the warlike array had disappeared.

A specimen of that even-handed justice dealt out by Captain Cook throughout the whole course of his arduous undertakings, and which gained for him the respect of the untutored beings by whom he was surrounded, may serve to show the character of the man, as well as that of the people of Tahiti. A native caught on shore, in the attempt to steal a water-cask, was sent on board, in irons, for punishment. There he was seen by the king, who earnestly entreated that he might be forgiven. This the captain refused, telling the king that as all offences committed by the English against the natives were strictly punished by their commander, it was only just that this man, who had tried to take their property, should be punished also. The fellow was forthwith taken on shore, and, in the presence of the king, his chiefs, and Captain Cook, with the marines under arms as a guard, tied up for punishment. Again it was tried to beg him off; but the captain, by his temperate though firm remonstrance, so effectually convinced the king of the justice of what was about to be done, that at last no more opposition was offered to it: Otoo contenting himself with the entreaty that the culprit might not be killed. As there had never been any intention of such a thing, this request was easily granted, and, the crowd being ordered to stand back, the thief got his two dozen in due form. When it was over, one of the chiefs addressed his own people, enforcing what Cook had said as to the justice of treating English and native wrong-doers alike, and he ended by begging them to mend their manners for the future. At the conclusion of his speech the marines were put through their exercise, including loading and firing volleys with ball; and with this expressive hint of what might happen if matters got worse, the affair ended.

Wood being wanted, the captain, with his usual consideration, asked leave to cut it, telling the king that he would not cut down any fruit-bearing trees. Otoo was much pleased with this, which he repeated to his people, and readily gave the desired permission; nay, in return for a kindly reception on board, with its accompanying presents, opened his heart so far as to tell the captain he might cut down not only as many trees as he liked, but of any sort that he chose, fruit trees and all.

The rough followed the smooth, as it usually does: some more stealing and enormous lying, both of which, alas! we do at home. But all ended well, thanks to the captain's invincible patience and justice; so, once more weighing anchor, they sailed from Tahiti, not ill pleased with the simple folk they had left behind, who, if they were no better than they should be, were not quite so bad as they might have been.

Their old friends at Huaheine, to which they bore direct,

anchoring on the 15th of May, were as well pleased to see them again as those had been from whom they had just parted. Hogs and red feathers were exchanged, the red feathers being held between the finger and thumb of the chief who received them, whilst he recited a prayer; and then everything was comfortable, with the usual drawbacks which always will occur where people, like our Society Islanders, are not perfect. One of their imperfections was rather amusing. Two officers went ashore to shoot, having with them bags full of the various articles used to trade with. These bags were given to two natives, who acted as guides, to carry, who, presently seeing one gun had missed fire several times and the other was just discharged, seized that moment to make off with the treasure, leaving the owners so confounded by the smartness with which it was done, that they had not the thought even to run after the thieves. Some other daring robberies were committed at this time, to the great disgust of the king, who was very desirous that the culprits should be punished for them: nay, he even suggested that they should all be killed with the guns; but as neither he nor anybody else could catch the delinquents, though a large party of English and natives gave chase one day, his excellent suggestion fell to the ground. Oree had begged to have an English force of twenty-two men to help him in the search, and the messenger whom he sent on this errand brought with him twenty-two pieces of leaves, lest he should forget the precise number wanted. This was their usual mode of assisting the memory. After the failure of the united thief-hunting, peace-offerings of plantain trees were brought by the chiefs, followed by so many good things in the shape of eatables, that though the expedition had not been successful in its particular object, the result of it was anything but unsatisfactory. The iron tiller of the pinnace, being stolen, was paid for in this way, and the exchange was thought a pretty good one.

When on shore in the afternoon, the chief was found at his dinner. In the first place a quantity of the root used for making ava was chewed by his attendants, and of its juice he despatched about a pint, almost at one gulp. Then he crammed himself—for they were hearty eaters—with plantain and other vegetables, winding up with a quart and a-half of the custard-like preparation of beaten breadfruit, plantain, and other things, that has already been described.

On leaving the island, October 23rd, Cook remarked to the chief that they should never see each other again, at which the old man wept, and replied, "Then let your sons come: we will treat them well."

On arriving at Ulietea, some of the gentlemen went on shore, and, to their consternation, were received at the chief's house by four or five old women, crying, and howling, and cutting themselves with sharks' teeth until the blood ran down; in which plight they insisted upon clasping the visitors in their arms, who could not, consistently with politeness, refuse. So, when they were well besmeared, the old ladies, being satisfied, cheered up, washed themselves clean, and then made themselves as agreeable as the best of them. It was simply their mode of greeting. Cook had a liking for the people of these islands, who had always treated him well—a little thieving was of no account —so that when sailing again, in a few days, he believed that the copious tears shed by the chief, his wife, and his daughter, were genuine ones, not done for effect. Oree would fain have persuaded his friend to return, but when he found that could not be, he asked Cook where his morai—that is, burial-place—was The captain answered, Stepney, that being the place where he lived when in London. He was made to say the word over and over again until they had got it thoroughly, and then the whole group of islanders repeated with one voice, "Stepney, *morai no Toote*"—Stepney, the burial-place of Cook. Another gentleman, who was asked the same question, replied that no seaman knew where he should be buried.

A young native of this island, a good sort of fellow, who had been with Captain Cook about eight months, and would fain have gone to England with him, but that the captain, knowing there would be no chance of ever sending him home again, had refused to take him, was now left behind here. But the poor lad almost broke his heart at the parting; so Cook comforted his soul by giving him a written statement of the length of time he had been with the vessel, and commending him to the notice of any who might chance to touch at Ulietea.

Thus ended, June 5th, the cruise of the "Resolution" among the Society Islands; the good ship now turning her bows westwards, to take what came in her way in the direction of the setting sun.

CHAPTER X.

NEW HEBRIDES.—NEW CALEDONIA.—LEAVE THE SOUTH PACIFIC OCEAN.

THE next few days' sailing did not afford much that was noticeable, except the discovery of a small reef island, to which our navigators gave the name of Palmerston, in honour of one of the Lords of the Admiralty. On the 20th land was again seen, and here Cook went ashore, hoisted his colours, and formally took possession. Actual possession, however, even for the shortest space, was briskly resisted; for a couple of natives, suddenly making their appearance, not only answered the friendly signs made to them by grim, defiant gestures, but flung a stone with such precision that it struck one of the gentlemen on the arm. The contents of a couple of muskets sent these to the right-about; and as the country was such a tangle of bushes that it was scarcely possible to get along, the party took to their boat again, and rowed along shore to seek a better landing place, which was at last found in a little creek, where four canoes were seen drawn up. It was an ugly spot in case of attack; but, as there were no natives in sight, Cook, having posted some of his people where they could keep a good look-out, went with a few others just to have a peep at the canoes, and leave a few medals and nails in them. All at once, down came an avalanche of infuriated savages, who, without staying to notice the friendly movement made by our people, set upon them like so many wild beasts, flinging their spears, spite of muskets humanely fired over their heads to frighten them. One of the spears so impetuously launched, flew close over the captain's shoulder, whose gun missed fire—these were not the days of rifles and percussion caps—otherwise the fellow who threw it would have been shot dead, for he was not five paces distant. Others, hastening to support their friends, were kept in check by musketry from the rocks where Cook had happily placed his men ; and under cover of this the whole party got safely back to the ship. It was plainly to be seen that there was no good to be got here, so they sailed away, avenging themselves by giving to this belligerent little bit of land the name of Savage Island. It was a singular speck in the ocean, apparently formed of coral rock, which the continual fretting of the waters had worn into fantastic shapes upon the beach. The natives that were seen were stout, well-made men, some of whom had the face, breast, and part of the legs painted black.

Steering west-north-west, after leaving these rough specimens of humanity, the group of the Friendly Isles was reached on the 26th of June, and Cook dropped his anchor in a sandy cove, on the north side of an island not previously visited by him—Rotterdam, or, as the natives called it, and as it now stands on the map, Anamocka. The people came off freely to him with yams and shaddocks, for which they got nails and rags. One man took a fancy to the "lead," and, in spite of the captain's threats, coolly cut the line with a stone; but some small shot, discharged in his direction, persuaded him to give it back. On shore things went on pretty well, the natives willingly helping our people to roll the casks to and from the watering place, on payment of a nail or bead for their trouble. There were mischances, certainly. The surgeon was robbed of his gun among them, and might have come to worse damage had he not had the wit to present his tooth-pick case, pistol fashion, at his assailants, who were overawed thereby, under the supposition, as it was conjectured, that it was the same kind of weapon as the one of which they had just taken possession, but of a smaller size. Unfortunately, no pains were taken to get the gun back; and, emboldened by this, these friendly folk next day snatched another, and made off with it, as well as several other articles. There was no standing this: so the captain proceeded to make such warlike demonstrations as speedily brought back one of the guns; and the other not following, he turned menaces into deeds by landing the marines, seizing two large double canoes, and sending one defiant fellow limping off with more small shot in him than was at all convenient to himself. This prompt action sufficed: back came the second musket, upon which Captain Cook instantly restored the canoes to their owners, and peace was patched up again. The natives asserted that the man who had been shot had died; and, to make good their words, brought him to the captain on a board, looking, indeed, as though he really were dead. To Cook's great relief—for there had been no wish to take life—it was soon found that he was only wounded; and the surgeon, being sent to attend to him, pronounced his hurts not dangerous ones: a present also relieved his sufferings, and reconciled everybody.

Meantime, the cooper's adze had been carried off by these nimble gentry; and as the captain had no mind to lose it, he applied with some energy, first to one, then to another, demanding its return. Among these, an old woman whose gifts of eloquence—or, at any rate, illimitable talk—had been conspicuous from the first, was exceedingly indignant at his conduct, telling him roundly, amid a profusion of words, that it was "mean" of him to make such a fuss about so trifling a thing. This was pretty good on the part of the old lady; but as she found that Cook cared nothing for her or her hard words—meanness, or no meanness, he was determined to have the tool back again—she concluded it was best to let him have his own way, took herself off, sent back the adze, and never came near him again.

One knavish fellow was dubbed by the crew, "Custom-house Officer:" for his way was to help himself to fruit or roots out of his neighbours' canoes, taking them by force, if resisted, and then to sell them on his own account. But though stealing was all fair and proper for him, he did not, it appeared, think it fair or proper for his neighbours; for, one of them playing off the same trick upon him, he darted after the man, gave him a beating, and brought back, not his own things alone, but many of those belonging to his victim and his friends. That fellow had a nice idea of restitution, where others were concerned.

Anamocka was left on the 29th; and, still sailing west, a

very small island was discovered on the 1st of July. It was named Turtle Island, from the great number of those creatures seen upon it, of which, indeed, they appeared to have sole possession.

On the 21st of July, after some baffling, stormy weather, the anchor was let go in eleven fathoms water, not more than two cable-lengths from the shore of an island previously discovered by the Spaniards, who had called it Mallicollo. The natives—dark, small, ugly, monkey-like beings—next day swarmed on board, so that even the rigging was full of them. They were vastly pleased with all that they saw; but a scuffle which took place with one who drew his bow on the boat-keeper, compelled the captain to give him the contents of his gun—luckily for the offender, small shot—twice over; and a flight of arrows from his friends was the result. A musket fired in the air was all in vain; but a four-pounder shot over their heads sent them flying in a trice, jumping out of the cabin windows, and overboard from the deck, to gain their canoes, or swim on shore. They did not, however, take this alarming mode of dispersing them amiss; for, on going ashore next day with an armed party in two boats, though four or five hundred natives, with spears, clubs, bows and arrows (the latter believed to be poisoned), were drawn up on the beach, no attempt was made to prevent the landing of our people; the captain first advancing alone, with a green branch in his hand: answering to our European white flag of truce. On seeing this, one of the chiefs, giving his weapons to another, came forward, also carrying a green branch, which he gave to Cook, taking his in return, and then leading him by the hand to the assembled natives, among whom his presents at once "made room for him." Wood was asked for by signs—for here, as in many other places, this was the only way in which they could make their wishes known—and leave given, in the same manner, to cut down what trees they wanted. A little pig was next presented by the natives, apparently as a peace-offering, for scarcely anything in the way of food could be obtained from them. Nothing that the English possessed, neither nails, nor even iron tools, seemed to have the slightest attraction for these strange folk; and as, in spite of the civil reception given to their visitors, it was plain that they heartily wished them gone, the latter retired as soon as they had got wood enough. It was rather odd that the unfriendly—perhaps it ought rather to be said unsocial—people of this island were the most honest that our navigators had yet come in contact with. A buoy that had been taken by them—and it was the only thing taken—was brought back, and put into the boat, without a word being spoken. And when the "Resolution" sailed again, which encouraged the natives to come off in their canoes for a little parting trade, several, who dropped astern after receiving the price of their articles of sale, instead of going off with it, and keeping their goods into the bargain, used their utmost efforts to overtake the vessel and send them on board. One man had a hard row for this, but a calm falling enabled him to get alongside, where he held up the article for which he had been paid. The thing had been forgotten altogether, so that several on board offered to buy it from him; but he refused them all until he saw the person to whom he had sold it, and to whom he now handed it. This person, who did not recognise him, offered something in return; but the man would not have it, holding up, in proof that he had already been paid, what he had received in exchange. Captain Cook remarks that their friendly, easy-going acquaintances in Tahiti, had not the slightest notion of honesty like this.

The women of the island were as ugly as their lords; and that is saying a great deal. By way of beautifying themselves, they coloured their heads, faces, and shoulders red. As, further, the bridge of the nose was pierced to receive a piece of curved white stone, some slight idea may be formed of the prepossessing appearance of the people of Mallicollo.

On the 23rd of July the island was left, as may be supposed, without the least regret, seeing that, in addition to the churlishness of its people, several of the officers were made ill by eating a poisonous kind of fish caught at Port Sandwich—that was the name given to their place of anchorage. The winds and waves now carried our voyagers somewhat north; and other islands were discovered, one small cluster of which Cook named Shepherd's Isles. Erromango, one of the New Hebrides, as the group among which he had been cruising for the last two or three weeks, was named, was reached on the 3rd of August, and on a landing being made, the people—tolerably well-featured, crisp-haired folk, with faces painted black and red—at first seemed well disposed towards him. But it was appearance only, for a very determined attempt to seize the boat was soon made—an attempt that compelled the captain to use his musket; but as the wretched weapon again missed fire, the savages were encouraged to treat him to a shower of stones, darts, and arrows. The marines had then to be called, and their first volley a little shook the assailants; though even that scarcely sufficed to drive them back, as from behind trees and bushes they continued to throw stones: whilst from time to time some more daring souls among them would peep out and launch their darts against the enemy. One of the crew was wounded, the dart being flung with such force as to penetrate his face to a depth of two inches, though the point was as thick as a finger. An ugly wound that! Of course it was up anchor and off, out of this wasps' nest; but before hoisting sail a four-pounder was discharged at the savages, which luckily frightened them quite as much as was desired.

At Tanna, south-east of the island from which they had thought best to make so rapid a retreat, Captain Cook made up his mind to stay for some little time, as he was much in need of wood and water. But here, too, he was obliged in the first place to frighten the natives into good behaviour, which being done, they settled down into very tolerable friendliness. A walk into the country gave our voyagers a notion of the natives' houses, some of which were open at both ends: all were thatched with palm. In front of most of the larger houses a framework of upright stems of cocoa-nut trees was set up for the purpose of drying the nuts; and the houses were usually placed under the shade of a large tree or two. The mode of clearing the ground for cultivation was very ingenious, considering their want of proper agricultural tools. The trees were lopped of their small branches; the roots were

VIEW IN TANNA.

then well dug under; and in the hollow thus made the loppings were burnt, together with the shrubs and plants that had been rooted up.

After the first difficulty had been got over, wood, water, fish, with some cocoa-nuts and yams, were had in a satisfactory manner. For a special piece of timber, wanted to mend the tiller, which had been injured, Cook saw only one tree that was suitable—a large one, which he desired his officer to fell, if he could get leave to do so; for he still adhered to his first plan of taking nothing without leave and payment: even the cocoa-nuts hanging here over the very heads of the workmen were as safe as though they had been miles off. It was understood that there was no objection to the cutting down of this tree, so the men were set to work; but, as it was a long job, before it was completed word was brought to the captain of the chief's displeasure at their doings. He stopped the wood-cutters immediately on hearing this; and then, seeking the chief, gave him a dog and a piece of cloth, explaining to him that their great steering paddle being broken, that particular tree was wanted to make a new one. The explanation, but more especially the present, was graciously accepted; full permission was given, and the tree came down in due course. There were, however, some troublesome, turbulent spirits here, that nothing could quell, chiefly among the younger natives; the older ones were more peaceably inclined.

The men of Tanna were lazy louts, without the least taste for work: they left the hardest of that for their women to do. They would not even give the slightest help to their foreign visitors in the work which was being done on shore, as the natives of the other islands had willingly done, for payment. As to their personal appearance, they had very dark skins, touched up as to the face, neck, and shoulders, with black, red, or brown; the hair, black or brown, and very crisp and curly, worn cropped by the women and boys; the men divided theirs into small separate locks, "got up" in the very ridiculous fashion shown in the illustration. They look like excessively small corkscrew ringlets; but the effect was produced by winding a narrow strip of some vegetable matter round each separate lock. The beard was bushy and short. Their dress was of the briefest. Their canoes and weapons were poor; the clubs were of several kinds, and from three to five feet long; their darts, which were thrown with the help of a short cord, after the manner of a throwing-stick, were cruel weapons, having three-edged, barbed points, but, though thrown with considerable force, were apt to go wide of the mark. The island itself was notable for a volcano, which at this time was in full action, throwing up fire, smoke, and great stones high in the air. An accident that occurred just as he was leaving Tanna grieved Cook exceedingly: a sentry, on some misunderstanding or pretence—it was hard to tell which—shot one of the natives dead. He excused himself by saying that a bow had been bent at him; but, alas! the slain man was not the one who had done it. Instead of resenting the act, as might have been expected, the natives about seemed simply terrified by it, for they ran off to their plantations, whence they brought cocoa-nuts to lay humbly at the feet of their dread visitors. It was a bad ending.

MAN, WOMAN, AND CHILD OF TANNA.

VIEW IN NEW CALEDONIA.

By the close of the month the remainder of this group had been briefly surveyed; and as, in addition to fixing with precision their situation and extent, Cook was also the discoverer of several of the islands, he thought himself warranted in giving a name to the whole, and New Hebrides was the one that he chose. They are very numerous, and lie between about 15° and 20° south latitude, and about 160° and 170° east longitude, being one of the larger groups of the Southern Pacific.

Returning south, to make again for New Zealand, where the commander intended refitting before having another dash into the Antarctic Ocean, our navigators kept their eyes open for anything that might be met with in the seas they were still traversing. They were rewarded by the discovery of another island on the 4th of September, and next morning a landing place was sought, not only for the purpose of seeing what the place and its people were like, but of observing an eclipse of the sun which was soon to take place. Large canoes were seen sailing about, but they paddled shore-wards rather hastily when two boats, with armed crews, put off from the ship to seek anchorage for her. This being found, she was soon surrounded by canoes mostly full of weaponless men, so shy that it took some amount of coaxing to get one canoe close enough to let down presents into it with a rope. The gifts were accepted, and acknowledged by a couple of fish, in the last stage of decay, being tied to the ascending cord. But as this miserable offering was meant well, it was taken well, and the natives, getting up their courage, soon came in considerable numbers into the vessel. They were all curiosity, examining every part of the ship closely. Goats, hogs, dogs, and cats, it seems they now saw for the first time, as all these creatures were so utterly strange that they had not a name for even one of them. Spike-nails, and pieces of cloth, especially if they were red, had their usual attractions for the savages.

Some came down to dinner in the cabin, but would not taste any of the foreign dainties—pease-soup, salt beef and pork—spread before them; contenting themselves with their accustomed yams, of which a supply still remained on board.

Cook went on shore after dinner, taking with him a native who had, from the first, stuck to him; and, with two armed boats' crews at his back, he was received in the most respectful manner. Scarcely even a stick was seen in the crowd before him, who listened in silence to first one, and then a second short speech, made to them by two of their chiefs, each sentence being followed by a grunt of approbation from the older natives present. Having asked for water, the captain and others of the gentlemen, being taken up the country to where it was to be had, came to a little straggling village, near which the ground was well cultivated, and laid out in plantations of sugar-canes, plantains, yams, and other roots, the whole being watered by small streams brought artificially from the parent stream, whose source was in the hills. There were cocoa-nut trees; cocks were heard crowing; some roots, in a large earthenware pot, of native make, were being baked over a fire; altogether, it was quite a bit of rural life in the wilderness.

MAN AND WOMAN, NEW CALEDONIA.

Next day their visitors came in swarms to the ship, but most of them empty-handed; for, indeed, there did not seem much to be had here, except good nature, of which there was abundance. But this was less the fault than the misfortune of the people of this island; for, with the exception of such spots as the village and its immediate neighbourhood, of which the utmost had been made, the country seemed a barren waste. Yet in this sterile region the botanist found ample employment and enjoyment, almost every day furnishing him with some new addition to his store.

The people appeared to be strong and active, friendly in disposition, and not at all addicted to thieving—an astonishing peculiarity among the islanders of the Southern Pacific. They were not generally ill-looking, though some had rather negro features; indeed, they are among those now known as Oceanic Negroes. Their frizzy hair and their beards were generally black; the former worn either tied up on the top of the head, tied in a large bunch on each side, or cut short: all the women had it cut short. Clothing was not worn, unless when they were doing nothing, or were out in their canoes, when some coarse matting did duty for it. A tall, cylindrical black head-dress appeared to be much prized, and appropriated solely to the great folks. Sheets of strong paper, got from the ship, were rolled up to form these by their fortunate owners. The women had a short petticoat, generally adorned with a few pearl oyster shells, fixed jauntily on one side, as you see a bunch of flowers, or some bits of lace and ribbon, stuck unmeaningly on one side of a European lady's ball-dress. Peaceable as they proved to be, they were well supplied with warlike weapons—perhaps it was the abundance of these that kept the peace among themselves—clubs, of different patterns, spears, darts, and slings, the stones for which were carefully shaped somewhat like an egg. Their houses, framed of spars, reeds, and the like, and thatched with grass, were like big bee-hives; the walls being raised only four feet and a-half, whence sprang a high conical roof, surmounted by a post, carved, or otherwise ornamented; occasionally there were carved doorposts. Upon the floors grass was spread, with some mats for the better sort, to sit and sleep upon. Two fire-places were common in these houses, and, as there was no chimney or hole for the escape of smoke, except the door, which was so low that entrance had to be made bent double, they were found by our people intolerably hot, as well as smoky. The natives seemed fond of warmth, making small fires here and there when they were out of doors, just to hover over and warm themselves. Three or four pointed stones, fixed in the earth outside the houses, served to support the cooking-pot over the fire which was kindled underneath it. The canoes were of the clumsiest make that Cook had ever seen. They were double ones, made of the trunks of large trees hollowed out—two, about three feet apart, fastened together by cross-pieces of wood, which projected a little over the side. On these was laid a heavy wooden deck, on which there was generally a fire burning, with cooking-pot at hand. The vessel was either driven by sails made of matting, or sculled, as it is called—that is, worked along with one oar

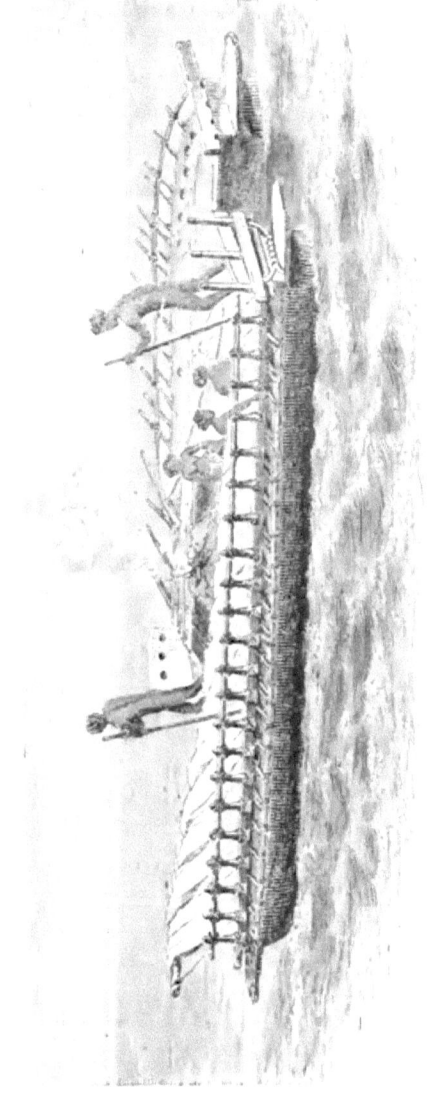

DOUBLE CANOE, NEW CALEDONIA.

or paddle. The ropes were made of twisted plantain fibre. These canoes were about thirty feet long, the deck not extending the whole length by some six feet. Their various parts were sewn together, the holes to receive the cord being evidently burnt in the wood; and as no instrument for the purpose was ever seen, it was conjectured that the eager demand of these people for such large spikes as they saw on board, in preference to mere spike-nails, arose from their desire to possess some more suitable tool than their own for the purpose.

As it was impossible to find out the name of this island, that of New Caledonia was given to it, as descriptive of its mountainous, sterile character. It is a very large one, more than 400 miles long, and somewhat narrow; in position it makes a sort of triangle with the northern extremity of New Zealand and the eastern one of Australia. Useful animals were left on shore here also, and were thankfully received.

After weighing anchor in Port Balade, some days were spent in exploring a portion of the somewhat dangerous coast of this island; and the "Resolution" had one or two narrow escapes from striking on the rocky shoals by which it is guarded. But she was well and smartly handled, and got off unharmed for her run to New Zealand, which was now her destination. A couple of albatrosses, shot on the 7th of October, and a porpoise, harpooned next day, made quite a feast for all on board, for they were by this time pretty well tired of living upon salt meat. On the 12th, land was seen south-west of their course, totally uninhabited, as it appeared, and to it the name of Norfolk Island was given—a name which has been spoiled to our ears, like Botany Bay, by its long association with criminals. The natural productions of this island were very like those of New Zealand, and growing in an abundance most welcome to our mariners, who brought on board as much as they could collect in their one visit to it. Some excellent fish were also caught off its coast. There was no break in the short voyage after this; and on the 18th they were once again snugly moored in their comfortable quarters, called by them Ship Cove, within Queen Charlotte's Sound, where their old New Zealand friends capered with joy at the sight of them.

There was much work to be done here, as the ship almost wanted turning inside out to make her fresh and strong for her coming campaign in the ice. But all went on well; and, after leaving some more pigs ashore—where they had the satisfaction of finding an almost newly-laid hen's egg, which proved that the former gift of poultry had not been wasted, though none were to be seen—the "Resolution," on the 10th of November, again stood out to sea, to make quite sure about the southern continent. Various kinds of weather were experienced in the course of this voyage: squally, hazy, "dirty" weather—which last is, perhaps, a compound of the other two—but, as there was no continent to be discovered, of course Cook could not find it. He therefore, on the 27th, decided to alter his course, leave the South Pacific Ocean, which he had thoroughly searched, and, steering direct east, try what the South Atlantic would do for him in the enterprise upon which he had set his heart.

NATIVE OF TERRA DEL FUEGO.

CHAPTER XI.

CHRISTMAS SOUND, TIERRA DEL FUEGO.—SEA LIONS.—DISCOVERIES IN THE SOUTH ATLANTIC.—AGAIN TURNED BACK BY ICE.—MURDER OF FURNEAUX'S BOAT'S CREW.—HOME.

IN addition to sweeping the South Atlantic, which was now his aim, Cook wished also to examine the coast of Tierra del Fuego—the Land of Fire, that is—which at that time was little known. It was a clear, uninterrupted run thither. From the 17th to the 20th of December was spent in exploring it—a desolate, dreary, savage-looking coast it was; and on the 21st, good anchorage being found in a cove, afterwards named by our navigators Christmas Sound, from their having spent Christmas-day in it, the ship was at once moored there. At the head of this cove there was plenty of wood; there was also a stream of fresh water, so that they could not have been more desirably lodged in this "fag-end" of South America. As they had, also, the good fortune to shoot some wild geese, abundant in the neighbourhood, they were enabled to have a jovial Christmas dinner, of which the varieties were roast goose, boiled goose, and goose pie; and their Madeira, got between two and three years before, being all the better for its keeping and its rolling about within the tropics, they did not do amiss, all things considered.

The inhabitants of this miserable bit of God's earth were as miserable as the country where they dwelt: ugly, dirty, half-starved, half-naked—spite of the cold, against which they did not seem to have sense enough to defend themselves, even by such means as were in their power. Two little babies were seen entirely naked—by way of hardening them betimes, one would suppose. Captain Cook was so distressed at seeing these poor half-clad wretches trembling with cold, as they stood on deck, that he gave them a batch of old canvas and some baize to wrap themselves up in. A party of them, including women and children, arrived in canoes made of the bark of trees: every soul of them smelling so strongly of train oil as to be almost intolerable to the not very fastidious noses of the English, somewhat accustomed, by this time, to what among civilised people is generally thought not to be borne. They were armed with bows and arrows, and had also harpoons, of bone, with which it was supposed they killed seals and speared fish. Some of them had European knives, gifts of which, and medals, pleased them highly.

The dwellings of these people were wretched structures of sticks and grass, through which wind, rain, and snow might have their free way. A few poles set up so as to meet at top, boughs and grass to cover these, with a hole left on one side for door and fire-place, made a Fuegian wigwam, and was not very unlike a bee-hive or haycock on a large scale. A little grass, littered down on the earthen floor, served for seats and beds ; other furniture, or cooking

FUEGIAN WIGWAMS.

utensils, they appeared to have none, with the exception of a basket to carry in the hand, and a bag or satchel to hang upon the back. Their bows and arrows were well made; the arrows, more especially, were the neatest Captain Cook had ever seen, being formed of highly-polished wood, with a bone or flint barbed point. What cruel weapons barbed arrows and spears are! Only think what it must be to get them out again when they have pierced their way into human beings!

As is often the case in dreary, barren lands, the botany of this portion of Tierra del Fuego was interesting, and abounding in variety, including beautiful and sweet-smelling flowers; so that again Mr. Foster, the naturalist, had a treat. Among its other productions was a species of duck, called by the sailors the "racehorse," on account of the swiftness with which it ran on the surface of the water, its wings being too short for flying.

Christmas Sound was left on the 28th, Cape Horn was doubled on the 29th, and at half-past seven that morning the South Atlantic was entered. Sending a boat on shore in Success Bay (on the eastern coast of Tierra del Fuego), where our navigator had been on his first voyage, search was made, in the first place, for any trace of the "Adventure," which, it was thought, might have preceded them hither. Finding none, a card, with the name of the "Resolution" written upon it, was nailed to a tree at their old watering place, for the chance of Captain Furneaux following them and putting in here. In truth, he had long been ahead of his old companions, having rounded Cape Horn in December, 1773. The natives about this bay, who were sensibly clothed in seal and other furs, were friendly, and seemed wishful for our people to enter the bay, which abounded with whales and seals. But there was other business in hand, so the vessel passed onwards. Fortunately, seals, or rather, sea-lions—as, from their likeness to that beast, our navigators called them, and the name has stuck to them—were not confined to Success Bay; for next day, coasting Staten Island, the anchor was cast near one of the islets flanking it, on purpose to send a shooting party to get some of this tempting fresh meat. They were in such numbers on the shore, that there was no difficulty in "stalking" the brutes; and they were also so stupid, that, like the boobies, they allowed themselves to be knocked down with sticks. The large ones were shot, for it was at first thought not safe to go near them. The old sea-lions were killed chiefly for their fat or blubber, to yield oil, the meat not being eatable; but the young ones were savoury. There were also birds to be had in this place of plenty: penguins (which, though not delicate eating, are better to some palates than "salt horse"), newly-fledged, tender shags, geese, and ducks; so that the boats returned laden with good things. A harbour, on the east coast of this island, affording plenty of wood and water to render it valuable to vessels doubling the Cape, received the name of New Year's Harbour, from the circumstance of its being discovered on the 1st of January. Sea-gulls were here in such clouds as actually, when disturbed, to darken the air.

There were numerous small islands close about, one of which, when our voyagers landed, presented to their

ICE OFF CAPE HORN

notice a sort of "happy family" of the wild beasts and birds by which it was peopled; all mixing together, like cattle and poultry in a farm-yard, though each had its own head-quarters. The sea-lions took the sea-coast; the sea-bears were up in the interior; the birds called shags perched themselves on the highest cliffs; the penguins liked to be able to run easily backwards and forwards between the sea and the land (their wings are too short to serve them for flying); and the other birds suited their tastes in their own way.

The sea-lion is a big, dark-brown beast, twelve or fourteen feet long; the neck, shoulders, and back of the head being covered with long hair, something like the mane of the animal after whom this creature was called. But they were most peaceable lions, not disturbing you if you did not disturb them. They might, indeed, raise their heads, snarl, and look fierce, if you waked them out of sleep—for that is what nobody takes amiably; but this was their worst fault, unless luckless wights chanced to come between them and the sea, in which case, if frightened, the whole drove would make no ado of running over you, in their mad attempt to get out of the way. The sea-bear is smaller than his noble brother, and has short, rather fine hair, of an iron-grey colour.

Staten Island was left behind on the 4th, and then they sailed right into the cold. An ice-encrusted island, discovered on the 20th, and named Georgia (now made useful as a whaling-station), had at first deceived them into thinking they had found the southern continent at last; but Cook was consoled for the disappointment by thinking that if this had been the object of his long and weary search, it would hardly have been worth the finding—if the whole were to be judged by the specimen. Georgia was soon passed, and they did a little more of that eccentric embroidery-pattern zig-zagging about among ice, and snow, and fog—for all of which that region is distinguished—until, on the 31st, a dreary, snowy, lofty coast was approached, to which, as the most southerly land yet discovered, Cook gave the name of Southern Thule. It was, in fact, one of a group of islands lying north and south, which he had discovered a few days before; and as he was not certain whether it was an island, or a bit of the long-sought continent, he named it Sandwich Land. A few days were spent in tracking the coast of this region of eternal snows, giving names to several of its more important points. And then his work here was finished. The Southern Ocean had been sailed over, from end to end—if we may so say of a circle— turning now to the right, now to the left, so that it was impossible that land of any magnitude should have escaped him. It was not simply that he had never seen land. The ocean itself had told him the secret; the shape and manner of its waves, both in the South Pacific and South Atlantic, from time to time saying, as plain as tongue could speak: "There is no large piece of land within hundreds of miles of us." And this tale, which none but a seaman could understand, had been told him so often, and in such various directions, that he knew it to be true of the whole expanse. He still clung to his idea of a southern continent; but he was now convinced that, if such there was, it must lie so near the Pole as to be perfectly useless to man, even if he could ever get there, which the captain more than doubted; for although, as we have said before, our means of getting a ship through the ice, as well as defending her against it, are greatly improved since the days of Cook, he had no ice-saws with which to cut a channel through the ice, should he unfortunately get fast ; nor was he either provisioned, or properly furnished in other respects, for allowing himself to be snugly frozen in until the returning summer should let him out. So, on the 6th of February, it was "'bout ship," in a very strong gale, and so heavy a fall of snow that the vessel had frequently to be so brought to the wind as to shake it out of the sails where it had lodged ; for neither they nor the ship could have borne the weight of it. There was an additional reason for turning back. With sails and rigging nearly worn out, and provisions so spoiled by age as not to have much good in them, it was time to think of home ; though the brave hearts of both commander and crew, if that had been all, would have carried them on still longer.

They now made straight for the Cape of Good Hope, and after being a few days on their homeward course, the captain, in accordance with his instructions, required his officers to bring to him all their journals and log-books, to be sealed up and delivered to the Lords of the Admiralty. They and the whole crew were further bidden not to tell any one where they had been or what they had seen, without permission from the same officials. But whether this procured for "My Lords" the first hearing of the marvellous story, they perhaps found out afterwards.

The Cape was reached in safety on the 21st of March, according to dates at the Cape. With Cook it was the 22nd, for in sailing round the world from west to east, a day is gained, and from east to west, one is lost; because, in the former case, each day begins a little earlier than the one before it, until at length, completing the circle of the earth, the time thus gained amounts to a whole day; in the latter this is reversed, until a whole day is lost. Cook had now to lose a day to bring him into agreement with the world about him, therefore he had the 21st March twice over. He was received here kindly and hospitably, with the exception of being made to pay exorbitantly for the repairs of the "Resolution," which, after being so long afloat in such very differing climates, were neither few nor small.

A letter was found here from Captain Furneaux, who had touched twelve months previously, on his way to England, giving a most distressing account of the murder of his boat's crew by the New Zealanders of Queen Charlotte's Sound, whom he had not been able to punish for their cruelty. It seems that a midshipman with nine men, being sent in the cutter to get wild vegetables for the ship, had been set upon, and every man of them destroyed by the savages, who, it was proved, had horribly eaten their victims, with the exception of some sad remains, which, folded in a hammock, were committed to the deep by their sorrowful comrades.

On the 27th of April, all repairs being finished and stores on board, the "Resolution," decked out in a complete suit of new sails (for the old ones were all condemned), left the bay, amid much saluting from and to the fort, and from a couple of foreign vessels that were also on the point of sailing. St. Helena was made on the 15th of May, and a few days were spent there on some necessary business. The Island of Ascension, between 600 and 700 miles north-west of St. Helena, was next called at. It is famous for its turtle, who are taken, when they come on shore, by turning them nimbly upside down, where, by reason of their size, they are rather more helpless than a beetle on its back; afterwards they are carried off leisurely in carts to tanks of water, in which they are kept until wanted. It was almost too late in the season for our navigators to be much the better for them, though they got a few of good size. The anchor was next let go at Fayal, one of the Azores, where the astronomer of the expedition wished to find out accurately the longitude of these islands. An attempt was made on the 19th to examine the coast of the Island of Terceira, which lay directly in their course; but it was defeated by the coming on of thick, hazy weather. Bowling along uninterruptedly after this, Spithead was finally reached on the 30th of July, 1775, after an absence from England of three years and 118 days: in the whole of which time, thanks to the captain's enlightened and persevering care of those under his charge, only one of the crew with which he had sailed had died from illness.

Honours and rewards awaited Cook, as was fitting. He was made a post-captain, the highest rank in the navy next to that of admiral. He also received a valuable appointment in Greenwich Hospital; whilst the Royal Society, of which he was elected a member, conferred upon him their gold medal, in special acknowledgment of the success that had attended his untiring efforts to preserve the health of those serving under him during this long and difficult undertaking: a success, important not to his own countrymen only, but to all, everywhere, "who go down to the sea in ships."

CHAPTER XII.

THIRD VOYAGE ROUND THE WORLD, IN 1776, 1777, 1778, 1779, AND 1780.—SEARCH FOR A SHORT PASSAGE BETWEEN THE NORTH PACIFIC AND THE NORTH ATLANTIC.—VAN DIEMEN'S LAND.—THIRD VISIT TO NEW ZEALAND.— ISLANDS DISCOVERED AND REVISITED.—GAMES AND ENTERTAINMENTS.—KING OF THE FRIENDLY ISLES.

SOME years ago we used to hear a good deal about the discovery of the North West Passage: that is, a sailing route from the North Atlantic to the North Pacific, going northwards of America, instead of the usual roundabout way past the Cape of Good Hope. This same short passage had also been sought by attempting to sail past the north of Asia; and that was called the North East Passage. It would have come to the same thing, as it was just like entering the same tunnel at different ends. Such a passage round the north of America, after more than three hundred years' search for it, was actually discovered in 1850 by Captain McClure; and when found, as might have been expected, it was also found to be quite useless, by reason of the icy difficulties that beset it and must ever beset it.

At the time of Captain Cook's return from his second voyage, public attention was much directed to this interesting subject of a shorter route to the East. Cook was not asked to take charge of the expedition to be fitted out for this purpose; but when he heard of it, it was quite in keeping with his character to offer himself at once for the service—an offer that was joyfully accepted by the Government, for there could not have been a better man for the work. His commission was accordingly made out: he was to sail in the first place for his newly-discovered or explored islands in the South Pacific, finding newer ones still, if he could, and then, turning north, force his way in that direction as far as possible between Asia and North America; when, if open water was found, he was to steer east, in the hope of coming out into the North Atlantic. This was seeking a North East Passage; and Cook had his own reasons for making the search in this direction, instead of the more ordinary one of east to west. Two ships were selected for the expedition: the old "Resolution" under Cook's immediate command, and with the same number of officers and men as on her last voyage; and a new one of three hundred tons burden, named the "Discovery," and commanded by Captain Charles Clerke, with a crew of seventy-nine men, officers included. Fresh presents of food-animals and garden seeds for the inhabitants of the Southern Pacific islands, were carried out by the commander on this occasion, and he was also well supplied with those various articles, which on the former voyages had been useful in trading with the natives.

As Tahiti was to be touched at, it was decided to

take that opportunity, the only one likely to occur, of carrying Omai back to his own land. He was glad to go home, and yet could not without regret leave a country where he had been treated with so much kindness, and had seen such marvels. His return was not empty-handed. The King, George the Third, and his other English friends, loaded him with all sorts of good things which it was supposed would be useful to him on his settling in his native land; and if he had only had a little common sense—which is by no means the exclusive possession of civilised people—he might ever after have been a prosperous, happy man, as well as a benefactor to his countrymen.

The "Resolution" sailed from Plymouth, and was fairly at sea by the 14th of July, 1776. Teneriffe was the first place touched at after leaving England. Next came the Cape, where Captain Clerke, who had sailed later, and had also been detained by a heavy gale, joined; and a short stay was made for refreshments. It was rather a disastrous stay, for, having landed the cattle that they might graze for a while, some dogs (there is scarcely a more useless or mischievous animal than an ill-trained dog) got among the sheep, worried four out of the sixteen, and so frightened the rest that they ran away, putting Cook to much trouble for their recovery; and, after all, two of them were entirely lost.

The Cape was left on the 30th of November. On the 12th of December, sailing south-east, two rocky islands were made out that had previously been discovered by the French; but as they had not been named by them, Cook felt himself at liberty to distinguish the two by the name of Prince Edward's Islands, in honour of the father of our present Queen. It was summer in this part of the world, though mid-winter in England; but such a summer! just as cold as our January; and some of the animals on board died in consequence. Sailing further into the cold, the two ships, on Christmas-day, came to anchor in a harbour of Kerguelen's Land, a dreary, desolate country, discovered by a French commander, whose name it bears; but for this Cook would have liked to give it the descriptive name of Island of Desolation, by which, indeed, it is also known. The bleak shore was almost covered with beasts and birds peculiar to a cold climate. Penguins were abundant; so were seals, of which they got as many as were wanted for oil; there was also fresh water, but not a stick of wood. This wretched land was coasted seven days for the purpose of discovery, and a sorry place it proved. Even in its most favourable part there was neither food nor shelter for cattle, so that, although they were dying on shipboard, it would have been useless to land them.

Sailing from this uncomfortable place, Van Diemen's Land was rapidly sped to; and on the 26th of January, 1777, the two ships anchored in its more genial waters. Wood and grass for the cattle were much needed, and both of these they hoped to get in Adventure Bay. But though the land was so much better than the one they had left, the natives here, who gave their visitors no trouble, were such poor creatures, that it was quite impossible to leave either cows, goats, or sheep with them. All that could be done for their benefit was to turn some pigs

ashore, who, according to their nature, would become wild at the earliest opportunity, and so take care of themselves. Bread, these wretched beings could not understand ; when it was given to them as food, they threw it away. Their appearance was far from being prepossessing. Their skins were a dull black, deepened artificially by some pigment that left its mark on everything they touched ; their hair, black and woolly, was smeared with red ochre; their clothing—well, some had none, and that of others was sufficiently scanty. Their habitations were like gigantic birds' nests—erections of sticks and the bark of trees, or singularly formed by hollowing out, to a height of six or seven feet from the ground, the trunk of a large tree, leaving one side untouched, so that the growth was not hindered. Inside the hollow thus obtained by means of fire, a fire-place of clay was made, and round it there was room for four or five people to make themselves comfortable. This was quite their best way of housing themselves. It may be observed that at this time Cook was not aware that Van Diemen's Land was an island ; he thought it a part of New South Wales. Bass's Strait, which separates the two, was not discovered until 1778.

The run from hence to New Zealand was not marked by any incident, save the melancholy one of a marine's falling overboard from the "Discovery" and being drowned—the second mischance of the kind that had befallen Captain Clerke since leaving England. On the 12th of February the vessels were safely moored at Cook's former station in Queen Charlotte's Sound.

The natives now seemed shy, and no wonder ; for there

was a bad conscience in the case: they feared the captain had returned to punish their cruel murder of Furneaux's boat's crew. But their fears were needless, seeing that Cook thought it best to take no notice of the crime: he told them so, after which their spirits revived, and the chief criminal put on all the airs of an innocent man. Cook was actually pleased with this conduct of his, which to us looks like consummate impudence. It is to be hoped the captain was right in his judgment; at all events, knowing the people as he did, and also the position of Europeans visiting them, he was a better judge than we, to whom it appears a grave mistake. But, though he did not think proper to avenge it, warned by the fate of that unhappy crew of the cutter, he took extra precautions against surprise by the natives during the whole of his stay at this time. The workmen on shore were always armed; marines were stationed on guard over them; and the ships' officers were never far out of the way: there was forgiveness, but no confidence. Omai, it must be said, was much dissatisfied with the lenience of the captain, whom he warmly urged to kill the guilty chief. "You tell me," said he, "if a man kills another in England that he is hanged for it. This man has killed ten, and yet you will not kill him." Some of the chief's countrymen would have been only too glad if Omai's remonstrances had prevailed, not so much to punish the murderers, but, as it seemed, to gratify private revenge; for, in their turn, the people of each village besought Cook to kill their neighbours.

Whilst the vessels lay here, there was so much to be done by the scientific men, and those unscientific ones, "hewers of wood and drawers of water," that it was indeed "all hands to the great cable;" and so entirely did the natives rely on the forbearance of their foreign friends that Ship Cove became the site of a suddenly-run-up New Zealand village: the huts being placed so thickly on the ground that there was scarcely room for even one more. It was a sort of gipsy camp, for these villages sprang up like mushrooms. A number of natives, bringing with them some of the scanty materials of their huts, would arrive in canoes, jump ashore, tear up the plants and shrubs on the piece of ground they had selected—or at once set up part of the framework of a hut, by way of asserting their claim to it—and in the course of an hour have their habitations complete; the women meanwhile looking after the canoes, or gathering wood for cooking dinner when the building was completed, which, hastily put together as it was, afforded sufficient shelter from wind and rain, both of which are prevalent in that country as they are in this. Our navigators were all the better for these villages rising up around, as it procured for them a good supply of fish, taken in abundance by the natives, who, in turn, were only too glad to exchange this for articles of English use. The New Zealanders also enjoyed another advantage from their neighbourhood to the wonderful strangers, inasmuch as it secured to them a plentiful supply of skimmings of the kettle and dregs of casks, throughout the time that converting seals' blubber into oil went on, with the crowning enjoyment of an occasional feast on the rancid oil itself. "Kings may be great," but these tattooed islanders "were glorious," when well filled with this greasy refection. The very lamps on board were emptied, wick and all going down with equal zest.

When about leaving the Sound, two native lads, bent on seeing something of the world and bettering themselves, were, at their own earnest request, taken on board to accompany that great man Omai to Tahiti; but, alas! when, towards the end of February, the vessels got fairly to sea on their way thither, the youths became terribly sea-sick, and, under the influence of that soul-depressing malady, heartily repented of their adventurous project. They wept copiously, and, waxing sentimental, expressed their sorrows in a kind of lyric strain, in praise of their native land, which they were leaving for ever. Perhaps this did them good. Sancho Panza says the grief that vents itself in the making of sonnets and madrigals is neither deep nor lasting, and assuredly his saying was made good in this case; as the boys' sea-sickness wore off they brightened up, and, as time wore on, they became thoroughly well content with their strange position.

During the short run from New Zealand to Tahiti an inhabited island was discovered, called by its natives Mangeea. They were tawny-skinned, robust savages, well armed with clubs and long spears. One of them who came on board, repeated a devout prayer or speech before he ventured to rope himself up the ship's side, and, once on deck, did not seem very happy in his novel situation. Poor ignorant fellow! stumbling over one of the goats, he asked what *bird* that was; nor was he the only one in those seas who took goats and sheep for birds. This island lies considerably to the north-east of New Zealand; but, as it had no anchorage for the ships, nor possible landing place for the boats, examination of it was out of the question. The land was tempting; but, like many other tempting things, it could not be got at.

The white wings of the ships were again spread, and, still sailing north, another island, called by its inhabitants Wateeoo, was descried on the 1st of April. The appetites of the beasts on board had never failed, so that green food for them was a constant want. Boats were accordingly now lowered to try for a landing here, and it seemed that the people of the place were equally well disposed to make the acquaintance of those of the floating houses—now first seen in their seas—for several canoes at once put off, and came alongside both the "Resolution" and "Discovery." These natives appeared unusually simple; they took the trifles given to them and offered cocoa-nuts in return, but, as it seemed, without the slightest notion of sale or barter. Invited on board, they were afraid of the horses and cows; as for the sheep and goats, they, like their neighbours of Mangeea, took them to be birds, so they did not mind them.

The surf made landing almost impossible, even for the boats, but with the help of native canoes two or three of the gentlemen got ashore, and met with civil treatment, though they had a dreadful fright on seeing a baking oven being heated; for, somehow or other, they took it into their heads that it was to cook them, and that when dinner time came they would be gobbled up by their savage acquaintance. Things, however, were not quite so bad, as it turned out that the roast was only pig, a sufficient portion of which, together with plantains, was hospitably set before them as they sat under the shade of cocoa-palms. It is recorded of them that fatigue had taken away their appetites; but our own impression is, that terror of being eaten themselves had on this occasion deprived roast pork of its usual attractions. Omai, who had gone on shore with the others, now came out in force. To magnify his friends was to magnify himself, and he did not stick at any amount of lying. He told the wondering natives that his pale-faced companions had ships as large as the island which they were now visiting, with guns big enough for several men to sit inside at their ease, and quite equal to crushing it at a shot. The guns on board the two ships, though small in comparison of those which his fertile imagination had invented on the spot, were, he further declared, also capable of destroying Wateeoo and every soul in it. The contents of a few cartridges that he had with him, judiciously popped off by a brand from the cooking fire, happily illustrated his lecture on the powerful weapons possessed by his protectors; and amid the flash, bang, and smoke of this bit of gunpowder, the cunning fellow towered over the simple folk around him like a giant among pigmies. All this was dreadful "gasconade" on Omai's part, but it not improbably saved his English friends from some inconvenience in this utterly uncivilised speck of earth. The officers of the "Resolution" could not have played Bobadil after such a fashion.

Wateeoo, which seemed a lovely, undulating, verdant spot, lies north, inclining to west, of Mangeea. The natives here had a singular way of paying respect to the memory of their deceased friends: they painted themselves all over coal-black, just as we put on black clothes. A neighbouring island, where landing was easier, was also more profitable to the voyagers, as they got cocoanuts for themselves, and green food for their cattle. Cook's former discovery, Hervey's Island, which was next reached, sent out a few unmanageable spirits, who, from their canoes, stole right and left, ingeniously using a long hooked stick with which to pick up "unconsidered trifles." But, as there was no anchorage here, stay was impossible.

Unavoidable delays of various kinds had now brought them to so late a period in the season, that Cook was reluctantly obliged to postpone for a twelvemonth the chief object of his expedition, that of seeking a short cut between Europe and Asia; and as water and fresh food for man and beast were much wanted, he decided to run straight for the Friendly Isles, where both might be had in plenty. A change of wind, however, compelled him to take Palmerston's Island in his way, and this afforded some refreshment both for his crew and his living cargo. On one of the islets forming the group, boobies were caught in abundance; and though not very tempting, were grateful enough to the palates of men long fed upon salt meats. Here, too, was a lovely coral bank, about which glided fishes of such beauty as to remind one of those in the *Arabian Nights*, of whom, despite their exquisite colours, it was asked sternly, "Fish, fish, are you in your duty?" A fine outside is no excuse for worthlessness within. The Friendly Isles were reached on the 28th of April, and on May-day the two ships cast anchor in Cook's old station at Anamocka. They were here visited by an important personage who was announced as king of the whole group—153 islands, they were told. In truth, he was no such thing, but he played monarch for a few days, and did it very well. On his approach, the natives went out to meet him, bowing down to the ground before him, and touching his feet with their hands, in a fashion rather inconvenient to the recipient of such homage. Fenou, as this chief was called, proved a useful acquaintance; for, in the first place, when he dined on board, so high was his rank that only one other chief was allowed to sit at table with him, instead of the swarms with which the captain was usually overwhelmed; in the second place, such was his power, that, on complaint being made to him of the stealing of a large axe, the tool was speedily restored to its owner. Such a state of things was all the more satisfactory, as the people of Anamocka had not at all mended their manners during the three years that had elapsed since Cook's former visit: incessant thieving was still their vice—a vice not confined to the common people, for upon one occasion a chief was detected walking off with an iron bolt hidden in his dress. Chief as he was, the captain forthwith had him tied up and treated to half-a-dozen lashes, just enough to make him very uncomfortable for some little time afterwards. The punishment was effectual as to his class; they had no more gentlemanly thieves. But by the lower sort the business was carried on as usual, and whether they had thicker skins than their betters, or less fine feelings, it is impossible to say; but, so far as flogging them was concerned, you might as well have flogged the main-mast. Captain Clerke at length hit upon the plan of shaving the heads of his thieves, and this made them look so ridiculous, even in the eyes of their own countrymen, that it was thought to be some slight check on the grievous nuisance; for it is a nuisance never to know when a thing is your own.

Some time was spent among these islands, the names of which it was perhaps impossible to get accurately; as, indeed, it often is of places at home, owing to the rapid, careless way in which people pronounce names or words familiar to them. At one of them to which our navigators repaired—after having, for the time, pretty well eaten up the first one—they were entertained with games and ceremonies, as well as with baked hog and yams. The captain, in the first place, received a formal invitation to come on shore. On arriving there, accompanied by Omai and the chief Fenou, he found a large assemblage of the people; and as soon as he was seated in a hut erected for his reception, the pageant began. A train of nearly a hundred natives was seen approaching, carrying with them yams, cocoa-nuts, bread-fruit, plantains, and sugar-canes, which were placed in two heaps on the visitors' left. Then, from an opposite quarter, came a similar train, bearing the same articles, who deposited their burdens on the right. Two pigs and six fowls were tied to these; to the former, six pigs and two turtles: a chief taking his seat by each group. The spectators were then arranged in a large circle, into which stepped men armed with clubs made of the green branches of the cocoa-nut palm, with which they fought a succession of single combats, until either their clubs were broken, or one of the combatants owned himself beaten, upon which the victor was greeted with shouts of applause. These were varied by wrestling and boxing matches; the latter being shared by stout girls, who went to work as coolly and as knowingly as the men. Half-a-minute, however, sufficed to put the first couple of young ladies out of fighting condition; the second, who seemed bent on damaging each other, had to be separated by two old women before worse came of it, for they struck with a will, as indeed all did.

When all the amusements were at an end, Cook was told that the larger pile of provisions was for him, the smaller for Omai; and that he might please himself as to what time he sent for them, as nothing would be touched. This liberal present filled four boats, and the captain made suitable returns for it, with which the chief was so well satisfied that he responded to them by an additional gift of hogs, fruit, and native cloth. The man had, at any rate, the spirit of a king.

Next day, by way of acknowledging the attentions he had received, Cook landed all the marines, and entertained his friends by their manœuvres and volley-firing, which afforded high gratification to the admiring spectators. Not to be outdone, the chief had this performance followed by a singular native dance, performed by a hundred and five men, carrying light paddles, which were waved and flourished in correspondence with every movement of their agile bodies, as the dancers glided about in rapid and intricate evolutions. English fireworks and more native dances succeeded; so that the visit was, altogether, a festive one.

Presently the real king made his appearance on the scene: a great man, certainly, for, though only about forty years old, he was almost shapeless with fat; but he was a respectable, sensible fellow, so his unwieldiness may be forgiven. On the approach of the "Resolution" to Tongataboo—the chief island of the group, and the royal residence—his majesty graciously accompanied her in his canoe, sailing round and round the slow-moving hulk, and running down two canoes full of his subjects with the most tranquil unconcern. It was like the donkey dancing among the chickens—"every one take care of himself!" Luckily, among these born swimmers, a ducking would be the worst that came of his majesty's sublime indifference. On shore he led the captain to a comfortable though small native house, agreeably situated within the fringe of the woods, and placed it at his service during his stay in the island. Poulaho—that was the name of the king—was friendly in the extreme towards his visitor, with whom he got very fond of dining; for he liked his host's wine, and, all unaccustomed to it as he was, could drink a bottle with ease, and be as pleasant during the time as though he had been used to it all his life. More dances were had here, in which the chief people themselves, including the unwieldy king, took part. Contests in wrestling, performed much as with us, each seizing his opponent by the girdle, trying to throw him on his back, and, if possible, spin him round two or three times first; and boxing matches, in which the blows were chiefly dealt at the head, also took place, solely for the amusement of their guests, to whom they sought to do all possible honour: while stealing their goods went on as briskly as ever. One clever attempt was made at noon-day to take an anchor from the very bows of the "Discovery;" and it would have been successful, too, but for one of the flukes getting entangled with some of the ship's gear, as the rascals were lowering it over the side.

Before leaving Tongataboo, Captain Cook made very valuable presents to its great men. To the king he gave a bull, a cow, and some goats; to others horses and sheep; for so ardent was the desire of the English Government—with the King at their head—and the discoverer of these islands, to make that discovery useful, that even such cumbrous beasts as horses and cows had been taken on board, in the hope of eventually furnishing the islanders with a race of these valuable animals. Pigs and rabbits were turned out to run wild, that being the best way of stocking a country with them. Some of the people seemed discontented with what they had got; and as, next morning, a kid and two turkey-cocks were missing on board, the captain, concluding they had been stolen out of revenge, determined at once to have them back. He acted with spirit as well as promptitude; for, in addition to seizing some canoes that bobbed up and down alongside, he went ashore, and, placing a guard over the astonished king, Fenou, and some other chiefs, told them they must remain in his power until all the missing property was restored. They seemed a little startled, but took it quietly, assuring the captain that turkeys, kid, and everything should certainly be brought back. Cook charitably took his prisoners on board to dine with him, but, getting most of the things back, released them, without their apparently retaining the slightest ill-will against him, for his capture of their royal and noble persons; for, even after this, feasts, with *kava*, as it is called here, and various entertainments of rare kinds, were provided for him and his companions at Tongataboo.

After the annoying circumstances just narrated, the king himself accompanied our navigators on a little excursion into the country, and gave them hospitable entertainment at one of his own houses: rather a large one, standing within a plantation, and having an extensive royal burial-ground adjoining. Large cypress-like trees shaded the grassy expanse in front of the house. Having lunched with the king, on their own provisions, brought from the ship, a long walk was taken under the guidance of one of the king's ministers, to whom they were indebted for keeping off the common people, who would otherwise have swarmed after the strangers. The chief further compelled all whom they met to pay to our people the same kind of homage as that due to the monarch himself: every man of them being commanded to sit down, just where he was, until they had passed. The country was found generally cultivated and fenced, with well-beaten public roads and footpaths intersecting it in all directions, so that the party got on with ease, returning at nightfall to the king's house, where a well-cooked supper of baked pig, fish, and yams was as ready for them as they were for it. Mats spread on the floor, with native cloth for coverlets, made very tolerable beds for tired men; and the king (who had been pleasantly if not profitably employed with his guests' wine and brandy during their absence) slept, like the rest, on his mat. Long before it was day, he and his native companions got up, and sat chatting in the moonlight; of course the talk was about their visitors, and the king was heard giving the wondering listeners an account of all that he had seen, and what he had thought of it. When morning had fairly broken, they went their way in various directions, but presently met again, bringing several others with them.

Without ava—or kava, as it is here called—the day could not be got through by gentlemen of the Pacific Islands; though the taste of it appeared to be so disagreeable to them that they gulped it down (like a dose of physic) with a wry face, and an apparent shudder of disgust afterwards. So, on the return of the king's friends, this nasty decoction was set in preparation, Captain Cook going meanwhile to visit a chief who had a remarkably good, well-kept house, close at hand, where that everlasting kava was also getting ready. This chief gave him a handsome present of pigs, yams, and cloth. By the time he returned, the king and his friends had got to the second bowl of their favourite drink; and, when it was finished, Poulaho invited his guests to be present at a mourning ceremony, which he was about to perform for one of his sons, who had died some time before. This turned out rather a disappointment to our English, who had expected to see something very curious or striking. The first part of the performance was the king's putting on a new piece of cloth, with a mat over it, old enough to have belonged to his great-grandfather: a couple of old women attending their lord in his dressing-room, which was the open air. The natives who accompanied him were also dressed in old mats, though not so old as that of their master: the older the mat, the greater the state, being apparently the rule on these occasions. Eight or ten men, having small green boughs round their necks, in addition to the ancient mats, then preceded the party to another house within a small enclosure, where, on entering, they threw their branches away, and sat down on the ground before the king, who had seated himself first. Others, also in old mats, came dropping in, until, the company being complete—numbering about a hundred—a five-gallon bowl of kava was prepared: drinking-cups being rapidly made of plantain leaves. The first cup filled was carried to the king, who sent it to somebody else. The second he drank himself, and Captain Cook got the third. After this, the man who ladled out the kava asked who should have each cup, as it was filled; and to the one named it was accordingly given. But, ample as was the bowl, it did not hold nearly enough for so large a company; so when it got low there were some anxious consultations between the native who handed out the liquor and those about him, as to who should have what was left. Yet, though half the assemblage were thus passed over, not the least annoyance was shown by any one of them: they were much too well bred for that. Half-a-dozen cups did duty for all, being thrown to the ground as soon as emptied, whence they were picked up, and taken to be refilled. While the drinking went on, the king and his immediate friends sat in silent gravity: scarcely a word was spoken among them. And this—kava-drinking, old mats, and the king's giving himself, according to their custom, a few slight blows on the cheek with his hand—made up the ceremony: disappointing enough to the sight-seers.

This liquor—simply the juice of the kava root, mixed with water—did not, apparently, produce any immediate effect upon the native drinkers of it; but some of the English, who ventured to try it, speedily found themselves in the condition of having taken a dose of opium.

Another solemn ceremony in the island, that one might express in English as that of the coming of age of the king's son, was only open to our navigators on condition of their stripping themselves to the waist, letting their hair (which, according to the fashion of the time, was worn long, and tied in a "pigtail," as it was called) flow loose, and sitting on the ground cross-legged, like tailors, with clasped hands and demure, downcast looks.

Whilst our people were rowing back again to the ship, after this little visit to the interior, Poulaho, who was in their boat, gave them a specimen of the way in which he exercised his kingship, by stopping two canoes, which he cleared of all the fish they had caught, great and small, giving some to Captain Cook, and letting his servants sell the rest on board. He afterwards ransacked two others, who, however, not having taken any fish, disappointed his majesty by not affording him anything. This seemed to be done merely as an act of kingly power, there being no want of food on board. In passing a large sailing canoe, everybody in it who chanced to be standing, at once sat down; even the steersman (who, by paying this homage to his sovereign and the foreign visitors, lost all command of his vessel) had to sit down like the rest.

On reaching the ship, it was found that two of the leading chiefs had on this occasion kept such order that not an article had been stolen during the captain's absence : which looked as if, had they always been in a mood to prevent theft, they might have done so. Good behaviour, however, was not particularly agreeable to these Friendly Islanders; so next day they sought to make themselves amends by setting upon a ship's party who were sawing planks. They were fired upon by the sentry, who hit one man with ball—as it was afterwards discovered—spite of the captain's strict orders to charge only with small shot. But who it was that (thinking himself so much wiser than his commander) had popped in that particular ball, was never known : the culprit not deeming it needful to inform against himself, whilst zealous friends were ready to swear that it *was* small shot after all. Three others of the assailants were seized, and punished before they were let go. This bit of unauthorised ball practice, however, did not turn out so badly as might have been expected ; for after it was discovered that muskets, in addition to spitting fire and making an alarming noise, could hurt them severely, the natives became less troublesome to our navigators than they had been : and to gain this our people could well afford to keep the wounded man in yams, and plantains, and the like, until his recovery, as they were made to understand it was their duty to do.

Mr. Anderson and Mr. King having made a separate excursion into the country, spent the night at a native house, where they met with a droll custom ranked among the luxuries of the great men of Tonga,—that of having servants to drum upon them with their fists while they slept. Two servants attended their master for this purpose; and they relieved guard, turn and turn about, so that one had a nap while the other drummed. After the great man was fairly got to sleep, they relaxed a little in their efforts, beating gently and slowly until he showed symptoms of awaking, when they instantly set to work—drum, drum, drum—as if for their lives, and soon had him off again. But though this curious performance put Tonga chiefs to sleep, the noise of it—drum, drum—kept English gentlemen awake; and as, in addition to it, the natives reposing around not only chattered at intervals, just as briskly as though it were broad day, but got up before it was light to eat a hearty meal of fish and yams, the visitors must have felt some longing for the comparative quiet of their ship's berth.

A few days before sailing, the king dined on board with Captain Cook; and the plates in use seeming particularly to attract his notice, he was desired to take his choice of one, pewter or earthenware. He chose a pewter plate, and then told his host the various uses to which he meant to put it. Among them were these: that in his absence from Tonga, visiting the other islands, he should leave this plate to represent him and receive from his subjects the homage they were accustomed to pay to himself. Formerly a wooden bowl, in which he washed his hands, sufficed for the purpose; but a bright pewter plate was certainly a more imposing representative of majesty. The wooden bowl had also fulfilled another duty, to which the pewter plate was thenceforward to be appointed. When a theft had been committed, and the thief could not be found, the custom was for the king, in the presence of his people, to wash his hands in the bowl, which, after it had been cleaned, was touched by them, one after another. If the culprit touched it, he died on the spot; any one who refused to touch it was known by that to be the guilty one.

The island was left on the 10th of July. A few days were passed at the neighbouring one of Middleburgh, to get water and fresh provisions; and here some sheep were put on shore, of which the chief, to whose keeping they were committed, seemed so proud, that it was hoped he would take good care of them. Melon and other seeds were sown, also, in the chief's ground; and having thus received, and, according to his noble nature, bestowed benefits, Cook weighed anchor, and on the 17th of July took his final leave of the entire group, among which he had spent between two and three months.

He had always thought well of the people of these islands, which had led to his naming them Friendly: not knowing that these civil, hospitable folk had been plotting to kill him, and take possession of his vessels.

They must have been clever hypocrites.

CHAPTER XIII.

OMAI AT TAHITI.—HUMAN SACRIFICES IN THE SOCIETY ISLANDS.
—COCKROACHES.—DEALINGS WITH THE NATIVES.

TAHITI was reached on the 12th of August, 1777, after some squally weather by the way, and the discovery of an island which there was not time to examine. The people of it, who seemed desirous that our navigators should land, spoke the same language as that of Tahiti.

On nearing their old anchorage in Oaiti-piha Bay, some canoes put off to the ship, containing, among others, Omai's brother-in-law, and some of his friends; but, on coming on board, neither they nor their long-absent relation and friend showed the least emotion, until Omai gave his brother a few of the red feathers which were so highly valued in the island. That entirely altered things: one of the friends immediately begged to exchange names with Omai, and was rewarded by a gift of these precious feathers from the latter, who, in return, received the substantial present of a pig. The news of red feathers being to be had spread like wildfire, and next day swarms of canoes surrounded the ships, in hopes of getting the coveted commodity in return for pigs and vegetables. Trade was brisk,

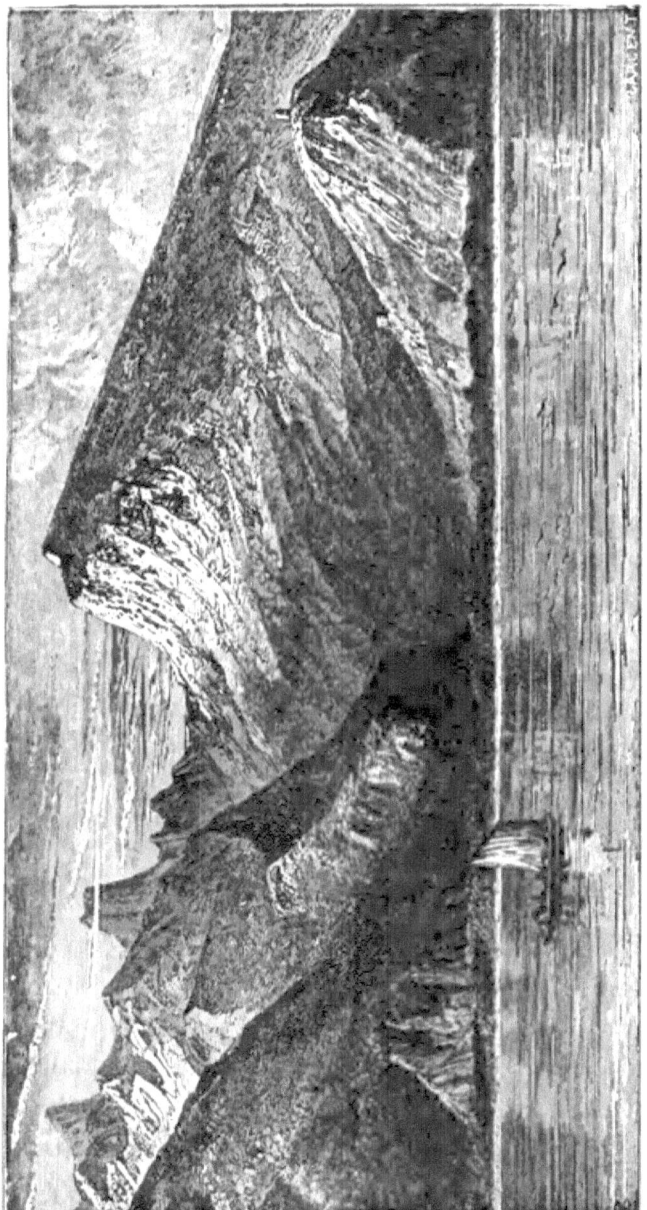

TAHITI.

and, at first, greatly to the advantage of our friends; for feathers—about as much as might have been plucked from a tomtit—sufficed for the purchase of a hog of forty or fifty pounds weight. But soon there was a rapid decrease in their value; for, alas! every one of the ships' crews had provided himself with red feathers, and so had the satisfaction of spoiling the bargains both of himself and his neighbours. Still they kept up a respectable value; they were the gold, so to speak, of Tahiti, whilst nails, beads, and other trinkets, once so eagerly sought, were now the smallest "coppers" of the community: scarcely any one would even look at them. Fashion was, and is, just as arbitrary and exacting in these uncivilised portions of the earth as in London or Paris.

Ship's work began immediately, for there was no time to be lost. Stores had to be got up and overhauled; ballast to be supplied in their place in the lower part of the vessel; and much caulking to be done, for during the voyage from the Friendly Islands the "Resolution" had leaked sadly. The cattle, also, had to be put on shore to graze during the brief stay here: there was plenty to do for everybody, and everybody did it heartily. The crew even consented to forego their "grog," save once a-week, in order to reserve the store of spirits for the cold climate which was presently to be their destination, receiving, in place of it, the abundant liquor of cocoa-nuts.

Poor Omai dressed himself up in a mixture of all the costumes, native and English, of which he had a scrap in his possession; and, entirely satisfied with the result of his labours, went on shore to visit the chief. This personage, who arrived on a handbarrow, accompanied his guests to a large house, where, his carriage being set down, they seated themselves by him, whilst much speech-making went on among the natives present, all tending to Cook's honour and glory, and to whom formal offer of friendship was made (including a polite gift of the whole province and its people), cemented by an embrace from the chief, and the exchange of their names, in correct Tahitian fashion. Simple, confiding, but headstrong Omai, spite of all his friend the captain could say, insisted on sending a present, made of red and yellow feathers, to Otoo, the king, instead of waiting to give it to him with his own hands; and the consequence was, as Cook had foreseen, that a very small portion of this rare gift ever reached him for whom it was designed, the messenger keeping the greater part of it for himself. But the poor fellow had no sense, or else his head had been turned by his new riches and dignity; and altogether he made such a fool of himself here as to forfeit the good will, not only of the king, but of all the chief people of the island. It was a great pity; for after his residence in England, and the many valuable presents with which kindly people there had loaded him, he might, had he had a little common sense, have been not only a person of importance in his native land, but a signal benefactor to it also. After the arrival of the ship in Matavai Bay, on the 23rd of August, more animals were landed; and seeds and roots were planted in a piece of ground cleared for the purpose, though Cook doubted whether the natives would ever take any pains to preserve them. An unwearying patience is required of those who would benefit savages or

OTOO, KING OF TAHITI.

uneducated persons anywhere; and this, we have said, our great navigator possessed in an eminent degree. His persevering labours, and those of others like himself, have borne fruit in the additions they have made to the settled comfort of the inhabitants of the Southern Pacific Islands, and to their usefulness as stations for provisioning vessels from far-off countries.

The people of Tahiti being at this time on the point of going to war with the neighbouring island of Eimeo, were very anxious that Cook should join them in their expedition. This, of course, was refused: he had no interest in their quarrels, and did not choose to make himself a party to them. As, however, according to their custom, they were about to offer a sacrifice to their god for the success of the undertaking, he took the opportunity of seeing, with his own eyes, in what the ceremony consisted. Otoo willingly allowed him to be present, and the whole party set out in the captain's boat for the morai, where the offering was to be made.

The sacrifice, alas! was a human being; for this was the horrible custom of these good-humoured, friendly Tahitians, Cook could not make out whether or not the man was a criminal who had been executed, but learned that such, or mere worthless vagabonds, were usually selected for the occasion. On reaching the morai, which was at once place of worship, of sacrifice, and of burial for the chiefs, and where four priests, with their attendants, were in waiting, the strangers were desired to take off their hats. The sacrifice—for the poor wretch had been already clubbed to death—lay, wrapped in cocoa leaves and small branches, in a canoe on the beach. The ceremony began by laying a young plantain tree before the king; then one of his feet was touched with a tuft of red feathers, tied, as has been mentioned, to a stiffly-twisted bit of cocoa-nut fibre. A priest, by whose side stood a man with two bundles of cloth, repeated a long prayer, at intervals of which young plantain trees were sent down to the beach and laid upon the sacrifice. After this, the plantains were removed one by one, and the sacrifice was taken out of the canoe and placed upon the beach, the priests surrounding it, whilst they recited various sentences, for the space of ten minutes. Another long prayer followed, the priests all holding tufts of red feathers, and then the victim, being carried nearer to the morai, was laid beneath a tree, where fresh ceremonies of a similar kind took place, accompanied by requests addressed to the dead that he would procure the delivery of the enemy and all his possessions into their hands. Finally, amid the slow, dull beating of drums, the sacrifice was taken within the morai, and buried in a grave, about two feet deep, dug at the time by some attendants. A miserable half-starved dog, brought with them for the purpose, was now killed, prayed over for a time by the priests, and then placed on a scaffold along with two other dogs and a couple of pigs, previously sacrificed. A shout was raised as the dog was laid upon the scaffold; and the ceremonies were ended for that day.

The natives gathered around did not seem to pay any special reverence to these religious mysteries. On the contrary, the great traveller Omai chancing to come up in the midst of them, he was at once set upon, and required to narrate his adventures, which proved much more entertaining to the auditors than the solemn chanting and offices of the priests. Captain Cook expressed his opinion of the wickedness of such a sacrifice very plainly to the chief who had prepared it, and who was very indignant at being told that if in England he had killed a man, as he had done here, he would have been hanged for it. "Vile, vile," was all the answer he made, nor would he hear another word. But his servants, listening to Omai's statements of what would be done in England, even to the greatest man, who had slain one of the very lowest, seemed to think otherwise than did their master; and that it would be a very desirable thing to have their own lives as well secured.

Otoo still remained the very good friend of our voyagers. After dining one day with Omai on fish, fowls, pork, and puddings, the captain waited upon the king, who had also been of Omai's dinner party, and found his servants busy preparing eatables to send on board. Among these was a large pudding, made of bread-fruit, plantains, *taro*, with palm or pandanus nuts, each shred fine, beaten up and baked by itself. When hot from the oven these ingredients were put into a wooden vessel full of cocoa-nut juice, along with some hot stones, and then the mass was well beaten together with sticks by three or four men until it was like hasty pudding. This pudding, which was excellent—it sounds so—and a baked hog, together with bread-fruit and cocoa-nuts, were sent on board the "Resolution," where the donor, with his family, helped the captain to eat it.

An evening or two afterwards, Captain Cook treated his

Tahitian friends to fireworks, with which they were more frightened than pleased: a "table rocket" dispersed the whole assemblage in utter confusion.

Next day a present was sent to him from the king in a very singular way: two girls had each so many yards of native cloth wrapped round her as to make the whole some five or six yards in circumference; and thus, nearly sinking under the weight, the two were brought on board to present it to the captain. The vast bulk was ornamented by native breast-plates.

Cook was, upon the whole, very well treated by his old acquaintances in this island, among whom he would have liked Omai to settle; but that unwise young man had a will of his own, so that his friend and protector had to take him away in the "Resolution" when Matavai Bay was left on the 30th of September. He finally established him at Huaheine, doing all he could to secure for him the good will of the people around, whom he further threatened with his heaviest displeasure—and the displeasure of one with a squad of marines at his back was a formidable thing—if Omai should in any wise be ill-treated by them. The taking this young man to England had been an experiment, the result of which was not very encouraging. Omai was not a bad man, but he was weak-minded, fickle, childish; and such are not of much use in this work-day world. He was in tears at parting with his friend and benefactor, though Cook's real friendship was such as it was impossible for one of Omai's character to appreciate. And here we bid farewell to the poor, foolish, though good-hearted fellow.

VALLEY IN HUAHEINE.

COCKROACHES.

Whilst lying in harbour at Huaheine, cockroaches—those pests by land and by sea—made themselves special pests on board the "Resolution." Ugly to look at, ugly to smell at, these disgusting insects went on as though they thought they had chartered the vessel for their own accommodation. If a sail was loosened, down they came in myriads upon deck. Nothing came amiss to their appetites: birds, stuffed and preserved as curiosities, were quite "game" to them; for writing-ink they had a passion, so that labels soon ceased to be of any use for indicating the contents of boxes and bottles, whilst books only escaped by the closeness of their bindings. Food of any kind was covered by them in a few minutes, and they messed and honey-combed it in a most sickening manner. The ship's bread was sadly damaged by these insufferably repulsive insects, of whom it has been said that they will regale, not only upon the strongest physic in the doctor's stores, but on the edges of razors and his surgical instruments. Getting rid of them was found to be impossible.

On the 4th of November, the "Resolution," having been towed and warped along, came to a safe harbour on the coast of Ulietea, being so laid as might best rid her of the rats with which she was infested: for rats are among the vermin which pester people on shipboard. The "Discovery" was going through the same process on the opposite side of the harbour. The chief, their old acquaintance Oree, received them with much friendliness; but they had some trouble whilst at the island, owing to desertions taking place. The first was a marine from the "Resolution," whom Cook's firmness soon got back again, and, fortunately, the circumstances were such that he was not obliged to be punished so severely as those shabby fellows, deserters, generally must be. Notwithstanding this forbearance—perhaps in consequence of it—in the course of the next ten days two others were reported missing. As Captain Clerke, to whose ship they belonged, sought them in vain, Cook was obliged to take the matter in hand seriously; and, accordingly, set out next morning, with two armed boats, in pursuit of the runaways. Not finding them, and suspecting they had accomplices among the natives, he quietly laid hold of the son, daughter, and son-in-law of the chief, telling the chief that he himself might go where he pleased, but his relations should certainly be carried away, if his people did not bring back the deserters. A dreadful howl was thereupon set up; canoes full of natives going under the stern of the "Discovery," where the hostages were detained, wailing, and lamenting, and, according to their custom, cutting themselves with sharks' teeth until the blood flowed. It was very unpleasant to be obliged to take such measures, but it was absolutely needful that they should be persisted in; and Oree, instead of joining the howlers, had the sense to hunt up the two worthless fellows who had caused all this disturbance. Meanwhile, he and his friends had prepared a very pretty counter-plot—that of seizing the captain, and then making their own terms for the release of Clerke's valuable prisoners. Cook's sagacity disappointed them in this little plan, and, the deserters being at last recovered, the family of the chief were instantly released.

Contrary winds detained them in this harbour until the

7th of December, when a light breeze springing up, the "Resolution," with the help of towing boats, fairly got out to sea, where she, with her consort, were once more launched on their voyage of discovery. A call was first made at the neighbouring island of Bolabolla, where, it was understood, an anchor, lost by a French navigator, was in the possession of the chief; and, as all the scraps of iron that Cook could collect had already been expended in traffic with the islanders of these seas, it was most desirable to get hold of this block of the precious metal, in order to strike fresh coin from it. A linen night-gown, a shirt, a looking-glass, some gauze handkerchiefs, beads, trinkets, and six axes, offered in exchange, readily procured its transfer to our friends, who, having got it safe on board, hoisted sail, and at once bore away northward, after having again left behind them food-animals to add to the stores of the islanders.

Cook was very anxious that the poor uncivilised beings with whom he came in contact should be permanently better, and not worse, for their occasional intercourse with Europeans. The beauty and fertility of Tahiti had attracted him; its inhabitants—with a merciful judgment of their imperfect character—he was, on the whole, pleased with; and as a good man he delighted in doing what he could to increase their comforts, and to raise them, in some degree, towards that civilisation which was, as yet, far off. And these feelings animated him and directed his conduct wherever he went—whether his poor savages were basking in the sun, as in the Southern Pacific, or cowering beneath winter blasts, as in the two extremes, alike freezing, of south and north.

CHAPTER XIV.

DISCOVERY OF THE SANDWICH ISLANDS.—NORTH-WEST COAST OF NORTH AMERICA.—NATIVES.

CAPTAIN COOK still continued to give fresh occupation to the map-makers. Those expanses of ocean which hitherto had been left almost blank, they were, by degrees, compelled more and more to dot over with islands of his discovery, single or in groups. On the 18th of January, 1778, pursuing his northward course, but inclining a little towards the west, land came in sight where none had been expected; and next day, whilst wondering whether it was inhabited or not, that question was solved by the appearance of some canoes, each containing several brown-skinned, stoutly made men, most of whom had their dark hair stained of a reddish brown. They paddled direct for the ship, but would not come on board, though they readily accepted little presents lowered down to them by a rope, sending up some fish in the same way in exchange. With the exception of a few small stones, they were quite unarmed, and these they threw overboard on finding themselves quite safe with the strangers. As the ships passed slowly along the island, seeking secure anchorage, the natives were seen crowding to the shore to gaze on the pageant; and other canoes came off, bringing pigs and fine potatoes, which were had on favourable terms, seeing that a sixpenny nail bought several of the former. But, oh, the value of a nail in such places! One of the Tahitian chiefs, being the owner of two large ones, made a comfortable living by hiring them out to his less fortunate neighbours.

Next day, several of those who had been hovering about ventured on board; and, accustomed as Cook was to notice the impressions made on savages by their first glimpse of civilised life, he had never been so surprised as he now was by the extraordinary astonishment of these poor creatures at all that they saw—it was plain they had never been in contact with Europeans before. Iron they seemed to have but a dim idea of, though they were aware that it was something that would act like one of their own hatchets. When asked what it was, they replied, "We do not know; you know what it is." When beads were produced, they asked what they were to do with them; were they to eat them?—for these were the only unornamented savages yet encountered. A looking-glass was equally unattractive. But, unusually ignorant as they were, they seemed to possess a sort of natural courtesy, asking where they should sit down, and might they spit on deck—a very uncommon degree of refinement this! Still, they were quite as ready as their more southern neighbours—whose language they spoke—to steal any article to which they took a fancy. A boat sent on shore, under charge of a lieutenant, to seek water and a good anchoring ground, was unfortunately set upon by the natives with such zeal—to help themselves to oars, muskets, and, in short, everything moveable in her—as to compel the officer to fire upon them; but this was not known to the captain until after leaving the island.

Suitable ground being discovered, both ships came to anchor, and several hundred natives being assembled on the beach, Captain Cook went on shore with three armed boats, and a guard of twelve marines. This imposing array had its due effect upon the wondering crowd, who all fell flat upon their faces and remained in that position until the captain made them understand that he wished them to rise. Upon this they gathered themselves up, presented him with young plantain trees, recited prayers or speeches, and formal friendship was contracted between the two parties. In exploring the island afterwards, Cook found its people fall down before him on his approach, this being, as he was told, their usual mode of paying homage to their own great chiefs. His walk into the interior showed him that the inhabitants were not without some knowledge of agriculture, in the cultivation of trees, plants, and roots, native to the place.

This island, called by its people Atooi, was one of a group—the islands in both Pacifics are generally in groups—to which our navigator gave the name of Sandwich Islands, in honour of the First Lord of the Admiralty, who had taken great interest in these voyages of discovery. In most particulars, including the frightful one of offering human sacrifices to their god, and that of eating human flesh—"savoury eating" one horrible old man called it—its inhabitants much resembled their neighbours of the Southern Pacific, already visited by Cook, though in force of character they appeared to be superior to those of Tahiti. Their cannabilism was placed beyond a doubt by the matter-of-fact question of a native, who, on being refused admission at one of the ports, simply asked if he should be killed and eaten in case he forced his way in; whilst his countryman, standing by, with equal coolness remarked that the strangers would be eaten if killed on shore. Morais, similar to those in Tahiti, were found here; and traces around showed too clearly that the ceremonies practised in them were of a like kind. The climate appeared to be more temperate than that of most tropical islands.

A brisk trade in pigs, fowls, and roots was opened at this place, and though the natives loved to steal when they could, to their honour be it said, they traded fairly. Among their articles of barter were some exceedingly beautiful feather cloaks and caps: the cloak, which was short, being made of a sort of net-work, to which red and yellow feathers were fastened, so as to give to the whole the appearance of velvet. The cap consisted of a frame of osiers and twigs, fitted close to the head, but rising into a crest, and had red, yellow, black, and green feathers closely worked all over it. The red feathers were obtained from a small bird of a vivid scarlet colour, with black tail and wings: great quantities of them were offered for sale. These rich articles of dress were costly, a musket being at first demanded for a cloak: afterwards, a large nail was sufficient for the purchase.

The natives, women as well as men, swam like fishes, jumping in and out of their canoes, and diving under them on the most trivial occasions. Even with their little babies in their arms, the women would (if the surf were too high to land the canoe) spring overboard and get to shore as composedly as possible: not because they did not care about their babies—for the poor little things were better taken care of here than in many uncivilised countries, where they are often of as little account as brute beasts.

These Sandwich Islanders were the only people of the Pacific Islands who did not pierce their ears for the purpose of inserting ornaments. They were content, like sensible folks as they were, men and women alike, with necklaces and bracelets: the former of bunches of narrow black cord with an ornament of some kind in front, strings of small shells, or the dried flowers of a native plant. Sometimes a little bone image, three inches long, was hung round the neck. The women's bracelets were variously made of shells, black wood, and ivory mixed, or the teeth of animals; those of large boar's tusks were very elegant. These ladies cropped their hair behind, and wore it long in front. The men stuck feathers in their hair, usually black by nature, but coloured according to the owner's taste, and dressed in various fantastic ways: shaved off on each side so as to leave a "cockscomb," or twisted into a number of little "pigtails;" for which, their own stock being insufficient, they added an extra supply of false hair, hanging, in this bewitching fashion, low down their brown-skinned backs. Their houses, looking not unlike haystacks, were constructed with poles, and neatly thatched with grass; a hole at one end or side served both for door and window. This was so low that you had to creep through it into the house; but the inside was found to be very clean. Strong coarse mats spread upon dried grass, with which the floor was thickly strewed, were used both for seats and beds. Their few household utensils were kept on a bench raised three feet high at the end of the dwelling, and consisted simply of gourd-shells, stained in different patterns, some of them being lacquered, and a few neatly-made wooden bowls and trenchers. Pork and fish—frequently salted down in gourd-shells—with sweet potatoes, plaintains, and the vegetable called taro, appeared to be the food of the people. Bread-fruit and yams seemed scarce.

All the articles of native manufacture were exceedingly neat and ingenious. Among these were their weapons: spears, of a fine chestnut-coloured wood, beautifully polished; daggers, some of them sharpened at both ends and held in the centre, so as to stab either way; and a few slender bows and arrows, which scarcely looked strong enough to be weapons of war: most likely they were for shooting birds. They had also knives of wood, about a foot long, set with shark's teeth; about as ugly a weapon as mortal could wish to be attacked with.

Of course these islanders—like the rest of the peoples of the world, civilised and uncivilised—played as well as worked. Their amusements were of various kinds: they sang; they danced in feather cloaks and caps; they had their games of bowls and quoits; and they soothed their perturbed spirits with such music as could be got out of a wooden and gourd-shell rattle, or two sticks, struck one upon the other, whilst the musician's foot beat melodious accompaniment upon a wooden platter turned upside down. To civilised ears the sound of such "music"—if it may be called so—would be nothing short of torture.

Cook did not see any of the chiefs of these islands, but one was brought on board the "Discovery," who conducted himself in the most helpless-grand manner imaginable. With a circle of his people joining hands around him, he stood stock still just where his attendants had placed him, on the gangway; and when he had had enough of it, was carried off in the same helpless fashion. He also royally ran against or ran down the canoes of meaner folk that came in his way, and who could not in the slightest degree help themselves, seeing that etiquette compelled them to lie down in their little skiffs until my lord had passed by.

Troublesome weather kept the commander beating about among these islands for some days; but, though the surf much interfered with landing, he managed to make out five of the thirteen now known to be their number, and which, for some years back, have been governed by one king (in place of the several chiefs of that time), having what may be called a parliament, something like our own, together with home ministers, foreign ministers, and law officers.

What would be the surprise of Cook, and his companions of less than a century ago, if they could revisit the scene of their arduous explorations!

Leaving behind him, as was his wont, various animals which it was hoped might make themselves at home here, our navigator hoisted sail on the 2nd of February, and, in company of the "Discovery," bore away still northwards. There was nothing to notice on the voyage until the 2nd of March, when a peculiar appearance of the sea, in which some small creatures were seen moving, induced them to draw up a bucketful for closer examination. Some of the more minute were placed in a glass with salt water, where, when at rest, they looked like little scales of silver; when swimming, which they did briskly, they threw out the most beautiful changing colours, such as those of a diamond or opal, and vivid enough to light up both the water and the vessel that contained it. By candlelight, their hue was a pale green, with somewhat of a golden tinge ; and even in the dark they emitted something of a fiery glow. It was conjectured that these little creatures were they to whom the phosphorescent glow-worm light, at times sparkling on the sea, or on the wet sea-sand, owes its existence : as had already been seen off the Cape of Good Hope.

How much beauty there is in the world ; but with scarcely anybody to enjoy it !

From small to great : whales were seen on the 6th ; and on the 7th, land, on the north-west coast of America, was sighted, one point of which received the name of Cape Foul Weather, to commemorate their discomfort from squalls, hail, and sleet, in its neighbourhood. Snow lay thick on the coast as they neared it ; and, altogether, it was wintry and disagreeable until the 20th of March, when they were thankful to cast anchor in an inlet of a more mountainous country than the one first seen : an inlet known to its people as Nootka Sound, but to which Cook, before becoming aware of that, gave the name of King George's Sound. This Sound is in what is now called Vancouver's Island: a name which it received from a midshipman of Cook's, in consequence of his, a few years afterwards, surveying the coast of this part of North-west America.

Three canoes put off to meet them as they neared this inlet. In one of them stood a round-faced, thickish-lipped, black-eyed native (rather more clothed than they had been accustomed to see their friends of the Pacific, but considerably dirtier than some of them), who, shaking a rattle in each hand, made friendly demonstrations towards the new-comers: speechifying and throwing feathers, whilst some of his companions flung red dust about. The speaker was dressed in the skin of some animal: two or three of the party had their heads strewed with small white feathers, as though a pillow-case had been shaken over them: others had large ones stuck here and there in their long, lank black hair. Altogether, they were an odd-looking set. One of these strange beings sang a soft, melodious air, which did not seem much in keeping with his rude exterior. Other canoes followed these, one of them having a singular figure-head, with an immense bird's eye and beak painted upon it. Its occupant, who vigorously shook a rattle which he held in his hand, was singular-looking also, being painted in a strange fashion, and having his head feathered to an extravagant degree.

Such were the men, short and plump into the bargain, who welcomed our voyagers to the north-west coast of America.

CANADIAN PINE.

Not prepossessing, certainly, but they turned out a tolerably decent set, for savages; being civil and good-tempered in the main—though suddenly blazing up if they fancied themselves wronged—and "indifferent honest." Yet such thieves as they had were much more dangerous ones than those our people had left behind; for they were possessed of good, sharp iron knives, with which they would whip a hook, aye, even of twenty to thirty pounds weight, off its tackle in an amazingly short time, and away with it. In trading, brass was greatly sought by them; and, seeing that our friends were getting rather low in the world as to articles for barter, before long they had almost stripped themselves of every bit of it, even to the buttons on their coats. What they got in return were furs of several animals: sea-otters, bears, wolves, deer, and others; dresses made of them; and a kind of cloth manufactured from the bark of trees, native weapons, and other little things fancied as curiosities: "Jack's" appetite for which at times gave his captain some trouble. The natives were keen bargainers, not suffering even what appeared waste grass to be cut without payment for it.

As the "Resolution" again required the carpenters to her, she was hauled up snug in the cove, and to work they went. Others of the crew set up observatories for the astronomers, cut wood, and prepared a watering place for the company in general; and brewed spruce beer (for everybody who chose to drink it) from the Canadian pines that abound here. Meanwhile, news of this important arrival upon the coast had spread in all directions, so that more than a hundred canoes, each containing, on an average, five wondering natives, thronged around our people in one day. Their manner of opening proceedings was by paddling strenuously round both ships; one, perhaps grotesquely masked, holding a spear or some other weapon, or only a rattle, in his hand, and shouting loudly— Captain Cook calls its "hallowing"—all the time. Then might follow a pleasing song with chorus: after which they quietly began business. So fond of masks were these people that one of them, having nothing better, stuck his head into a tin kettle he had got on ship-board; and made a sort of Mambrino's helmet of it.

Bad weather and other disagreeables made the ships' work lag; but on the 19th of April, Cook, beginning to see an end to it, took a walk to examine the neighbourhood. The people (whom he well knew) of a large village now reached, received him in a very friendly manner, each one cordially inviting the captain into his house, where a mat was laid for him to sit down, and other marks of respect were shown to him. Most of the women were at work, either making bark cloth, in precisely the same way that the New Zealanders made theirs, or curing small fish by smoking over a fire and then pressing them close down in bales. Their houses were poor places, about seven or eight feet high, built of planks tied together by strips of pine bark: the pine and the white cypress were the principal trees of this country. Doors, properly speaking, there were none: any accidental gap, caused by the unequal length of the planks, served as an entrance; or, if this was wanting, one was made on purpose. Holes, with a bit of mat hung over them to keep out rain, did duty for windows. These buildings were mostly large, and divided into compartments for different families, something like a stable with two rows of stalls: a slightly raised bench at the side, covered with mats, served for sitting and sleeping. A huge piece of tree-trunk, clumsily carved into something of a human figure, and supposed to be of a sacred character, was frequently found within them. The fireplace was in the centre, and had neither hearth nor chimney; so it was no wonder that the poor, greasy, bepainted inhabitants were shockingly dirty. Furniture was comprised in a number of chests to hold the family valuables; and these were often ornamented with much ingenuity. Wooden cups, buckets, and shallow troughs to eat out of, lay or hung up about the house in like confusion with their fishing tackle.

The canoes were exceedingly light, and even the largest of them, holding more than twenty people, were formed of a single tree; they were managed by paddles only, for sails were unknown.

Among the savages hitherto seen, broiling and baking were the only modes of cookery practised, owing to the want of suitable vessels for boiling or stewing. Here, however, they managed this latter, by placing, with a cleft stick as tongs, hot stones, one set after another, in a wooden bucket containing the meat and water. One may, perhaps, imagine the flavour produced by such a process, no matter what might be the meat of which soup was to be made. Porpoise was seen cooked in this manner.

It was well the "Resolution" had been put into good sailing order in Nootka Sound, for on leaving it, on the

26th, so severe a storm was encountered that, even as it was, she sprang a leak. After some hours baling, however, one pump kept it under, and she pursued her course, still north-west, in hopes of accomplishing her great design: her captain carefully examining the coast whenever the wind was not so violent upon it as to render approach too hazardous. Cook was a cautious as well as an enterprising man: rashness is no part of bravery.

Land was again made May 12th, for, though the leakage was kept in check, it was very important to stop it entirely, which they had been unable to do at sea. This was an inlet on the main coast, and to it Cook gave the name of Prince William's Sound. The natives were like those of Nootka Sound, but cleaner, and also apparently more disposed to fight. Their canoes were made of seal, or other skin, stretched over a slight wooden frame; and in these they paddled to within some little distance from the ship, when they drew up shouting, alternately clasping and spreading out their arms, and then joining in a song. One man held up a white garment, which was taken to be a flag of truce, or peace; another, without a scrap of clothing on him, stood up in the canoe motionless, and with his arms stretched out like a cross; but whether that meant peace or war, was not in itself very evident. Feathers tied to long sticks were likewise held out; but, though gestures of good will were made in return, none ventured on board until some of our people got into one of their canoes. Among those who, after that, summoned up courage enough to come on deck, was their chief, a good-looking middle-aged man, dressed in sea-otter's fur, and wearing a cap ornamented with small light-blue beads, upon which he set a high value. Beads were very attractive to these people; iron also was much desired, provided it was in large pieces, not less than eight or ten inches long, and two or three broad; for small ones they would none of. They behaved very well, and left in the course of a few hours, going straight on board the "Discovery." Their good behaviour, however, was deceptive; for just after they had gone, a boat, being sent on shore to sound for a more suitable anchorage, was seen by them, and they at once left the "Discovery" and made towards it: a movement which induced the officer to return. The whole of them followed him, and on his stepping on deck, leaving only two men to keep the boat, immediately attacked it. Several of them jumped in, and whilst some threatened the two sailors with their spears, others cast off the rope by which the boat was secured to the ship, and tried to tow it to the shore. Bold, however, as was the attempt, the moment they saw preparations for resisting their design they let their prize go, got into their canoes again, and, as coolly as though they had done nought amiss, made signs to those on board to lay down their arms. On board the "Discovery" they had been more impudent still, for, finding only an officer and one or two more about, they drew their knives, making signs to those on deck to keep out of the way while they betook themselves to plunder. A boat's rudder lying loose was seized, and at once thrown into one of the canoes alongside, before any one had time to stop them; but the alarm caused a pretty scramble on deck from below, and the crew, armed with cutlasses, caused the whole set to retreat, which they did with provoking calmness, quietly explaining to their comrades in the canoes how much longer the English knives were than their own.

In person these natives were rather under-sized, but they were strongly made, with thick, short necks, and broad, flat, swarthy faces, having something of a frank, good-humoured expression. They dressed themselves in a sort of frock, reaching to the knees, or ankles, made of various skins of animals, furry side out; or of birds' skins, from which the feathers had been plucked, leaving only the down underneath. The seams of both kinds of garment were ornamented with leather tassels and fringes: comfortable and handsome dresses enough. In wet weather a waterproof, made of the intestines of whales, or some other large creature, was worn over all; and the lower part of it being tucked tight around the opening in which they sat in the canoe, kept out sea-water, as well as rain-water, to perfection. Stockings were rarely worn, though some had them; but mittens, made of the skin of bears' paws, were almost universal. When the head was covered, it was with a high, half-conical cap of wood or straw.

The plain faces of these northern savages were made plainer still by their ugly fashion of wearing what the sailors had already dubbed "spritsail yards"—that is, a bit of bone, or other substance, thrust through the centre of the nose; and that of dividing the under lip in such sort that the first of our people who saw it called out that the men had two mouths. Ornaments of various kinds were placed in this slit; and as, by way of completing their personal attractions, they frequently painted their faces

SAVAGES' ORNAMENTS.

bright red, black, or blue, some little notion may be formed of their hideous appearance.

We laugh, or are shocked, according to our mood, at these poor ignorant creatures for making holes in their very flesh for the purpose of sticking in what they think ornaments; but, as long as European ladies are content to do the same thing, we perhaps have not much right to do so. There is no such great difference between the ear, and the nose, or lip, as to render perfectly rational in the one what is preposterous in the other.

In their dress and habits, the people of this Sound were much more cleanly than those of Nootka. Water seemed to be their only drink; they were seen to take it in mouthfuls of the snow with which their country lay covered all the year round. White seal-skins, beautifully spotted with black, were common in this neighbourhood.

The stormy condition of the weather prevented Cook's seeking a better situation for the repair of his ship, so the anchor was let go here; when a very singular accident befel one of the sailors, who, getting entangled with some of its tackle, was carried by it to the bottom, whence he presently came up again, having skilfully disengaged himself from the heavy mass: bringing, however, a badly broken leg with him. How astonished all must have been to see his head above water, after going down in such company!

By the 17th the leak was effectually stopped, and the sheathing replaced; so there was nothing to prevent the captain's putting to sea, except the difficulty of picking his way out of this unknown Sound, amid sunken rocks and other difficulties of navigation. Careful examination of it by the boats enabled him to do this safely; and by the 19th he was once more in open water, prepared to search in higher latitudes for that passage into the North Atlantic which he was never to find, and in connection with which he speedily had a severe disappointment—a promising inlet being traced far enough to discover that it was only a great river, instead of, as hoped, communicating with either Baffin's or Hudson's Bay, which would have solved the long-perplexing problem. This river was named, after its explorer, Cook's River. The country on its banks was, in the usual manner, taken possession of for us English.

The two ships continued their tracing of the north-west outline of North America, giving names to leading points or islands, either first seen by them, or imperfectly known and unnamed before, until the 19th of June, when their monotonous life was startled by the firing of three guns by the " Discovery," which also signalled to speak with her consort. Taking for granted she had sprung a leak, or met with some other accident, Cook immediately sent off a boat to her, which as speedily returned, bringing Captain Clerke to make his own report on the matter. It seemed that some canoes had followed him for a time, and at length, coming up with the ship, a native, who took off his cap and bowed after the manner of Europeans, on a rope being lowered to him fastened to it a small wooden box; after which, with other signs and unintelligible words, he went off with his companions. What the man said or meant was not at all understood, so the stupid captain did not at once open the box. When he did, it was found to contain a piece of carefully folded paper, written upon in foreign characters, supposed to be Russian. It was dated 1778; and Captain Clerke, conjecturing it to be sent by Russians, who had been shipwrecked on this coast, and desired his assistance, was anxious to give them immediate succour. Cook differed from him entirely; and, taking for granted it was simply a note of information from some Russian trader in these parts, left with the natives for them to hand to the first ship of his nation that arrived out, and by them, in mistake, given to the English, decided on disregarding it, and passing on without delay along the coast, continent, or islands—he did not know which—as it might be.

From what occurred afterwards, he was probably right in his decision; but the man's manner showed that he must have been in communication with Europeans, and the hope of meeting some of these was not otherwise than cheering to our navigators, who had for so long a time had no intercourse, outside their own ship, with any save savages, many of them both disgusting and brutal.

In a few days afterwards, just as they had had a good and most welcome catch of halibut, communication with these partly Russianised natives was again had; for a small canoe, containing one man clad in unmistakably European style—green cloth trousers and black cloth jacket, under his waterproof—and who bowed and capped like the former one, came up with some neatly-made bone harpoons, and a fox skin, for barter. For his own refreshment by the way, he had what appeared to be a bladder full of oil—a travelling-flask, let us call it—from which he took a drink, after the manner of other travellers with their flasks, and then fastened it up again. His little canoe was impelled by a double-bladed paddle—that is, one having a blade at each end—with which the water was struck rapidly, first on one side, and then on the other, of the boat. Nothing, except trade, could be made out of him, so he went his way.

A few more days' sailing brought the ships in sight of an island, which, they found, was called Oonalashka, the natives of which were well behaved, though rather shy. One of them—who got a ducking by the canting of his canoe, which was carried adrift—on being picked up and brought on board, conducted himself like a gentleman: going into Cook's own cabin, when invited to do so, in an easy, unembarrassed manner, and dressing himself in the English clothes given to him by the captain in place of his own wet ones, as though he had worn such things all the days of his life. The dress under his waterproof was of birds' skins, with the feathers innermost. This, next the skin—for our shirts and flannel waistcoats are things unknown in those regions—must have been rather luxurious. Another Russian note was presently brought on board by a native; but as nobody could read Russ, it was unintelligible, like the first.

CHAPTER XV.

ANCHOR ON THE COAST OF ASIA.—NATIVES.—ARCTIC ICE.—
SEA-HORSES.—RUSSIAN TRADERS.—SANDWICH ISLANDS.—
OWHYHEE DISCOVERED.

PUSHING their way still to the north, our navigators reached the extreme western point of North America on the 9th of August. It was very far north indeed, and on its opposite shore, only about fifty miles off, was the extreme eastern point of Asia, which is called East Cape. Of course, Behring's Strait, which is the name of the sea between these two parts, was known before Cook's visiting this region; but it was not known, previously to his ascertaining it, how very narrow was the watery space that separated the two continents: so narrow, that we may believe that the two were once one. And, indeed, all the world over, shores thus slightly separated generally, by the sameness of their structure, of rock or soil, show that the separation has not been from the beginning. On this coast, opposite to the one he had so long been following, Cook anchored on the 10th of August; and having already seen upon it a village, and inhabitants apparently alarmed by the sight of the ships, he went on shore to see what they were like. Three armed boats formed his escort on this occasion, and as they neared the shore some thirty or forty men, armed with highly-ornamented iron or steel spears and bows and arrows, with quivers slung over the left shoulder, were seen drawn up close to their village, and fully prepared to receive the visitors, friend or foe, as it might turn out. Three of these advanced, taking off their caps, and making low bows; but the moment the boats put ashore they retreated, as if in a fright. Captain Cook, unarmed and quite alone, followed and came up to them, and at length friendly gifts were exchanged between the two parties, though which began it the captain could not afterwards recollect. From this interview he brought away a couple of fox-skins and two sea-horses' teeth. The people appeared to be exceedingly timid; but his efforts to gain their confidence were to some extent successful, and a little traffic took place for beads, knives, tobacco, or such things on one side, and native dresses and arrows on the other. The arrows, either stone or bone-pointed, were not generally barbed. Some had blunt points, and it was conjectured that these were designed to kill animals without injuring the skin.

These people seemed to be of a race entirely different from those seen on the American coast, and also superior to them. They were clothed in frock, trousers, boots, caps, and gloves of leather, extremely well dressed, some with the fur outside, others having it within. They had also dog-skin hoods, covering both heads and shoulders.

The village, which had been seen from the ship, comprised winter and summer habitations. The former were somewhat sunk in the ground, and overhead were framed of wood and the ribs of whales, put together and covered with earth. The summer dwelling was a large round skeleton of bones and slight wood-work, with a covering of some sea animals' skin, and having partitions of skin to accommodate the various members of the family. Deerskins were used for bedding, and these were mostly clean and dry, though their cooking and eating utensils were dirty enough. Many large, long and soft-haired dogs were seen about : used, it was supposed, to draw sledges—many of which were laid up in the winter huts—and also for food.

These people were called Tschutski, and, after a short stay abreast of their forlorn country, possessing neither tree nor shrub, so far as could be made out, our navigators passed over towards the American side of the strait; thence bearing northwards, slightly inclining west, in pursuit of their great object. In a few days the keen air and gloomy sky indicated their getting near the ice region, and, sooner than was expected, that peculiar brightness in the horizon, known to arctic men as the *blink*, announced their immediate approach to it. An hour or so afterwards they found themselves "brought up"—as they had been when going towards the South Pole—by a field of ice that there was no penetrating, nor even flanking ; their attempts at the latter only bringing them, on the 18th of August, in face of a wall of rugged ice, twelve feet and more in height, extending east and west as far as eye could reach.

Here, as in the essay south, in the absence of ice-saws and other modern contrivances for contending with frozen obstacles, it was again "No road this way;" and Cook, though prepared to grapple with any difficulties, was too good a seaman to contend with impossibilities. His object was not to make a name for himself, but to do his work; and when this, spite of all the efforts that could be made, proved impracticable, he had resolution and self-denial enough to turn back. It was not solely his own life— such a man would have thought little of that, as would every brave man with a good conscience—but the lives of near 200 other men that he had in charge; and these he was bound not to risk in what, if pursued under the circumstances in which he now found himself, would have been a "wild goose chase."

An ice-covered point of land about three or four miles ahead of him, in about latitude 70°, descriptively named Icy Cape, was therefore the limit of Cook's advance north; for the lateness of the season made it hopeless to seek for any other passage into the Atlantic.

With ice about him, and sea-horses, as they were then called—now known as walrus—disporting themselves on it, whilst his crew was in want of fresh meat, an attack upon the beasts was at once decided upon, spite of an announcement from some of the more knowing of the crew that they were not fit to eat. However, after some of them had been shot, it was found they were not quite so uneatable as had been supposed—for hunger, like necessity, has no law; and so it came to pass that even sea-horse was received as an acceptable substitute for that "salt-horse" of the sailors, which, by reason of long keeping, and being the only fare on board, was by this time anything but either tempting or wholesome. Well was it for the crew that they were all in health, for even "dog" might have been unattainable here to meet the delicate appetite and support the wasted frame of an invalid. The walrus were not so bad, after all, though the lean of their meat was coarse, black, and rather strong. The fat was more agreeable, but soon spoiled unless salted. Their skins, being exceedingly thick, were very useful for rigging and the like.

The sea-horse—or walrus, to give it its modern name—is a species of seal, of vast bulk, armed with enormous and most powerful tusks, shooting downwards from the upper jaw, with which it will break up even the strong granite-hard arctic ice with apparent ease. These animals were seen lying huddled together in large droves upon the ice-fields, and roaring so loudly that their noise made our navigators aware of the nearness of these frozen plains and heaps. When collected in herds in this manner, some were always stationed as sentinels, who, while the rest slept, kept awake in order to give the alarm if danger were suspected. Then the whole herd would leisurely take their huge bodies out of the way, unless they were fired upon, in which case they would with all speed tumble one over another into the sea. For these big brutes were rather timid, diving at once at the bare flash of a musket, though a mother-walrus would defend her young one to the last, were it upon ice or in the water. Why this animal should ever have received the name of sea-horse is hard to say, seeing that it has not the least resemblance to a horse. The conjecture that sea-horse is a corruption of its Russian name, *Morse*, seems therefore a very probable one.

Returning was a matter of no small difficulty amid the accumulated ice, which not only rose above the level of the sea, but sank to an astonishing depth below it. These difficulties and others were, however, successfully overcome, and, adding to our geographical knowledge as he proceeded along —keeping nearer to the Asiatic coast—Cook was able, by the 3rd of October, to anchor safely in a bay of Oonalashka, one of the Fox Islands, a dreary, barren, prolonged cluster in the North Pacific, about on a line with Kamschatka. The natives of this place—where the Russians had a settlement for trading in furs—supplied our voyagers so well with fish, dried and fresh, as to make a considerable and very important saving of the ships' stores; whilst the health of the crews was also benefited by the cranberries, whortleberries, and others of the kind, growing in profusion, which they were allowed to go on shore and pick. Cook never lost an opportunity of either doing or permitting what might contribute to the health and comfort of those under him.

The Russian traders, discovering that Europeans were in their neighbourhood, opened communications with our people by sending them a couple of salmon pies, with rye-flour crusts, one for each captain, together with a letter, which, being like the former ones, in Russ, could not be read. The kindly present was, however, acknowledged by sending to the donors a few bottles of rum, wine, and porter; whilst an intelligent corporal of marines was despatched with the messenger to make out these Russians, if possible, and let them know that his party were friends and allies of their nation. This man, Lediard, soon returned with three Russians, who, so far as they could be understood, seemed very friendly, as did another of superior rank, who made his appearance a few days afterwards. This gentleman, whose name was Ismyloff, arrived in a small canoe, attended by a number of the natives in theirs, who on landing immediately raised a small tent, brought with them, for their master, and then rapidly constructed others for themselves, with their canoes and paddles for framework, covering the whole with grass, so that the party were housed at once. Mr. Ismyloff invited Cook to visit him, and gave his guest the best cheer in his power, which was only dried salmon and berries. But though there was but sorry means of hospitality, there was the spirit of it, which is its best part, after all. Spite of the difficulty of intercourse where neither understands a word of what the other is saying, information, both interesting and useful, was had from this gentleman; and the interchange of visits with him and his companions proved an agreeable variety in the life of our own people. The former were found living under one roof with some natives of Kamschatka and those of these islands, who were servants of the Russians; the latter taking for their share the upper end of the house, the Kamschadales the middle, and the natives the lower end, where was fixed a large boiler for cooking. Their food was coarse of its kind, but the Russians, being good cooks, managed to make even whale pleasant eating. Bread or flour was almost unknown among them; wine, beer, or spirit they had none, water and the juice of berries being their only drink. What a treat, in that cold region, the captain's little present of wine and porter must have been! The procuring furs, chiefly those of the sea-beaver and otter, was the motive for settling in this disagreeable country.

The natives of the island, cheerful and frank among themselves, were most inoffensive to others, and extremely honest; but it was supposed to be the result of their Russian masters having given them some severe lessons. In person, they were short, plump, and not ill-made, having full, swarthy faces, with the usual ornaments of ear-rings, and pieces of bone stuck through the under lip; the eyes were black. Their long, lank black hair was worn by the men cut short in front and hanging loose behind; the women tied theirs up in a knot. Men and women dressed alike in long frocks, with a waterproof, having a hood made of birds' skins drawn over it, for the former, of seal-skin for the latter. All the men had wooden caps, dyed of various colours, and adorned with long bristles upon which glass beads were threaded. They were very fond of tobacco and snuff; the former was chewed, as well as smoked. Their houses were most miserable, dirty places, usually entered from the roof by means of a post with notches cut in it for steps. Cooking they did not much trouble themselves with, generally eating their food raw, though some of them had the foreign luxury of a little brass kettle, and those who had not, made one of a flat stone with standing-up sides of clay, like a "raised pie." The houses were warmed, not by fires but lamps, formed of a stone like a large dinner plate, hollowed on one side to contain oil, with dry grass for a wick. The women were eminently working women, making all the clothes and shoes, and even the skin covering of their boats, with a bone needle, and fibres of split sinews for thread. The canoes, in which they tucked themselves up warm and dry, were driven by the double-bladed paddle, smartly, and in a straight course, at a rate of even seven miles an hour. These canoes, which were the smallest our voyagers had seen on this coast, were about twelve feet long, one and a-half broad, and twelve or fourteen inches deep, and would, in case of need, carry two persons, one lying at full length, the other sitting in the usual opening, around which was fixed a piece of waterproof skin, that could be drawn together at the mouth by strings, like a bag; this, when the paddler was seated in the canoe, was brought up and fastened round his body, to prevent the entrance of water—any that might make its way in was taken up with a sponge carried for the purpose. The canoe was of seal-skin, stretched over a slender frame of wood; the hunting and fishing implements—made of wood and bone, for they had no iron, and did not seem to want it except for sewing-needles—were in readiness upon the canoe, secured in their proper places by straps. These implements were handled with remarkable adroitness in spearing fish, both at sea and in the rivers.

The ships remained in this harbour until the 26th of October, when they weighed anchor, hoisted sail, and started away for the Sandwich Islands; it being Captain Cook's plan to winter there, and return north in the summer, to renew that search for the North East Passage which overwhelming ice had suspended for the present year.

Instructions were accordingly given to the commander of the "Discovery" which might guide him, should the ships get separated as before. That "Discovery," from some cause or other, was, throughout, a more unfortunate vessel than her consort, and she was soon in distress again; for, before very long, in the midst of a severe gale, she was heard firing guns—which at sea always means mischief. The "Resolution" answered her; but the storm, which drove the "Discovery" out of sight for twelve hours, prevented any communication between the two for several days. When, at length, Captain Clerke managed to come on board, it was to report that his firing had been to signal the serious damage he had sustained from the storm; and also that, almost immediately after leaving the harbour, he had lost one man, killed, and had had three or four hurt, by the giving way of a portion of the ship's tackle.

The Sandwich Islands, to which they were bent, were sighted on the 25th of November—not any of those with which our navigators were already acquainted, but first one new one, called by the natives Mowee, or Mauï, and then, on the 30th, another, the largest of this group, Owhyhee—or, according to its more recent spelling, Hawaii—was discovered. To the surprise of those on board, its mountain tops were seen covered with snow; for they had no idea of the loftiness of their peaks, some of which tower up more than 13,000 feet above the level of the sea.

The island was skirted for between six and seven weeks, during which time its coast was thoroughly explored; and the ships received from the natives—who were thought friendly, reasonable, and confiding, treating their visitors with much respect—the usual and very acceptable supply of fresh provisions: fish, pork, and vegetables. They themselves also ate dog, but that was not a marketable article with our people. These people of Hawaii seemed superior, as to strength and activity, to those of the Friendly Isles, and of less pleasing appearance than the Tahitians. But they were far from ill-looking savages; their chiefs and great people being generally handsomer than the lower class, though many of them were disfigured by the effects of ava-drinking—the peculiar privilege, fortunately for the rest, of the great folk—which seemed to half paralyse the whole body, as well as injuriously affect the skin and eyes. A twelve-year-old son of the king used—poor little wretch!—to point out with glee a small spot on his side, the first indication of this pernicious drink's having taken hold of his constitution. The lad was actually proud of it!

The Hawaiian dress was, of course, as usual in all the islands of the Southern Pacific, next to nothing, though rather more than the negro's cocked-hat and shoes. On very great occasions their chiefs appeared in the beautiful cloaks and helmets, constructed of feathers, that have already been described. Here, the rank of the wearer fixed the length of the cloak—from reaching to the waist, to trailing upon the ground. Why is it that, all the world over, clothes of undue length should be taken as a sign of dignity? Is it to give an imposing idea of always having some one to wait upon and help the wearer? The inferior chiefs had their cloaks not only short, but made of less costly feathers; still, they were of brilliant hues, with here and there a few formed exclusively of white ones, with a coloured border. Their mats were used for defensive armour only, for which their strength and thickness well adapted them, and were too cumbrous for ordinary wear. They were manufactured from a plant whose leaves resembled those of the pine-apple; were beautifully wrought for strength, beauty, and fineness, and were stained of various colours. The mat was generally five feet long, and four broad, and it was put on mantle fashion. These people lived in villages of from one to two hundred houses, set down anyhow, with no attempt at order, but having a path through them; and they appeared to get on well enough among themselves, though the chiefs were always ready to rule each other, with a rod of iron, whenever they got the opportunity.

Among the amusements popular in the island was one not unknown among ourselves. It was played between two, one of whom placed a small stone under a cloth, which he afterwards so rumpled and crumpled that it was impossible to tell where the stone lay; the other then, making the best guess that he could as to its whereabouts, struck with a stick the spot where he imagined it to be. If he was right, he won; if wrong, he lost. And as they were all gamblers by nature, the chances of this simple game gave opportunity for the bystanders to make any amount of bets, as to the result, that they had a mind for. Their bets were apt to be heavy. One man was seen tearing his hair, and beating his breast, in a fury at having just lost three iron hatchets, bought on ship-board at the price of half of his possessions, through betting at a race between boys and girls.

KAKAKAKOOA BAY, OWYHEE.

A species of cup and ball, or rather *spike* and ball, was a great favourite with the children, and certainly required no small skill to play it successfully, the ball being thrown up, and caught on the sharp point of the peg, to which it was tied, as in our own game; whence it was instantly flung again, and caught on the opposite end of the peg: and so on without once missing.

Their weapons of war were spears, clubs, daggers, and slings. The spear, of hard solid wood, was either six to eight feet long, with a four or six-barbed point, or twelve or fifteen feet in length, simply pointed. The dagger, or *pahooa*, was of a ponderous black wood, one to two feet long, and secured to the arm by a loop. The clubs were of all sorts and sizes; the slings were of the invariable form of that weapon.

The general impression made by the people and country was exceedingly good; and so delighted was Captain Cook with the discovery of this large and beautiful island, varied by mountain, and plain, and stately forest, that he, as well as others on board, were now only too glad that circumstances, felt at the time to be very annoying, had driven them to seek shelter and refreshment among the Sandwich Islands.

An anchorage suitable for the purposes of his intended stay among the group was at last fixed upon; and our voyagers, with hundreds of natives swimming like fish around them—plunging and diving, as though the sea were their natural element—canoes hovering about, and a beach crowded with wondering lookers-on, were safely moored in Karakakooa Bay, on the western coast of Hawaii, on the 17th of January,

1779. This bay was about a mile deep; its shore, dangerous for landing in bad weather, except at the spot selected for anchoring, at its northern extremity, where the ragged black coral was exchanged for a fine beach of smooth sand, and there was also a well of fresh water. Its centre was filled up by a tall grove of cocoa-nut trees, with a large village near at hand.

CHAPTER XVI.

Ceremonies at the Morai.—The Taboo.—Chiefs.—State Visit of the King.—Funeral of a Sailor.—Leave the Island, but compelled to return.

IN coming to this island to gain sustenance and strength for future toil, our great navigator had come to his death. But he did not know it. It was, perhaps, well that he did not; for, though he was not a man to slack in his active duties, even in the face of death itself, the knowledge would have weighed upon him, and rendered those duties more oppressive; whilst to one living as Cook did, in the diligent discharge of all the duties of that state of life to which God had called him, death, perhaps, cannot come amiss. This, of course, is said without reference to those internal convictions and motives to duty which give to duty its right character, as judged by God; and of which, as in Cook's case, and many others, having no knowledge, we cannot take account. But where the life has been so pure, and good, and actively beneficent, as was his, we are bound to suppose the motives also pure and good; and that Cook, in the performance of his duty, was serving God as well as man.

Two chiefs were met with at this bay, with whom our navigators had at once made friends. Cook had strikingly the art of attaching men, civilised or savage, to himself—generally a sign of goodness, or greatness, or of both, as in this case; and these two, one day, brought on board with them a third, a feeble little old man, named Koah, who was announced as a priest. Koah, approaching with much reverence, first threw around the captain's shoulders a piece of red cloth—their sacred colour—and then made a formal offering to him, in somewhat the manner of a religious ceremony, of a small pig, which he held whilst pronouncing a long set speech. This ceremony was afterwards repeatedly performed towards Cook during his stay in the island. Its exact meaning was not known, but it was evidently to do high honour to its object. When the speech was ended, Koah dined on board heartily; though, like his countrymen generally, he could scarcely be persuaded a second time to taste either wine or spirit: one sip of the nauseous stuff was quite sufficient. In the evening, Captain Cook and two of the officers went on shore with him. On landing, they were received by four men, carrying wands tipped with dogs' hair, who walked before them, making some kind of proclamation, in which the word *Orono*—a title of great dignity among the islanders—was alone understood; the natives, almost to a man, retreating from before the procession, the few who remained throwing themselves on the ground in its presence. The group passed on to the morai, a solid pile of stones, fourteen feet high, whose flat top was surrounded by a wooden railing, upon which were fixed the skulls of those sacrificed on the death of chiefs. On reaching it, the party were led up to this platform, at the entrance of which were hideous wooden figures, or rather posts with grotesquely carved heads, the shapeless trunk being wrapped with red cloth. Here some ceremonies were gone through, and at the end of them Cook was taken underneath a lofty stand (placed before another figure), supporting various fruits and vegetables, and a hog in the most odious state of decomposition. The hog was held out towards the poor captain all the time that another long speech was being made; after which it was thrown to the ground, and the priest, Koah, led him to a crazy, tumble-down erection of wood, on which the two clambered together, at the risk of coming down again rather quicker than they went up. Another offering of live pig and red cloth was made here, the cloth being first wrapped round the captain, who, in a somewhat perilous position from the ricketty condition of the scaffolding on which he sat, had to listen to a long chant, poured out by the priests. At its conclusion, this hog, also, was let go, and allowed to fall. The captain was then liberated, and led down again by old Koah, who snapped his fingers and said something, apparently in contempt, to each one of a half-circle of wooden figures, with the exception of that in the centre, which, in the sacred red cloth, met with more respectful treatment, being kissed, and fallen down before, by the priest, who successfully requested the captain to follow his example. This falling down on the face, it must be remembered, was the usual mode of doing homage to the king and great chiefs.

Entering another part of the morai, Cook was next

seated between two wooden figures, one of his arms being supported by Koah, the other upheld by Mr. King, who, with the others, must have had much ado to keep a decently grave face throughout the performance; and then preparations for dinner were seen at hand: baked hog and pudding, with the customary supply of roots and vegetables. But before it could be eaten, the pig was, in most reverential manner, offered to the guest whom it was intended to honour, amid chanting of the priests, dying away in the single word Orono. Poor Cook's troubles, however, were not even yet at an end: evil-smelling pig, ricketty scaffolding (perilling his neck, or less important bones), and other nuisances, were not enough; for, before he was permitted to attack the excellent fare provided him, one of the priests chewed a piece of cocoa-nut, put it into a piece of cloth, and then smeared it over the face, head, hands, arms, and shoulders of the unfortunate captain. Further, in order to do their visitors the utmost honour that it was possible for Sandwich Island gentlemen to render, the meat, after being pulled in pieces, was put in gobbets into their mouths by the attentive chief and priest. Mr. King stood this, for his feeder was a man remarkable for his cleanliness; but poor Captain Cook, who had fallen to the polite attentions of Koah, not having got that horrible *bad* hog out of his head, was too sickened to swallow a morsel, notwithstanding that, to make it go down the better, the civil old priest had *chewed it for him!*

Truly, honours are at times hard to bear; and those of us who do not get them may (especially if uncivilised countries should be their scene) be thankful for our insignificance.

At the conclusion of the banquet—a Barmecide one to him for whom it was specially designed—presents were given to the natives; and the little party returned on board with the same ceremonies that had attended their coming ashore.

Cook has been blamed for joining in these ceremonies; but it is a question not worth going into. Even if he was to blame, which of us is perfect? The wisest and best at times commit errors of judgment.

Another half-religious ceremonial, of which our English were the subjects here, proved an exceedingly useful one. This was the *taboo*—a sort of interdict, laid by the priests upon any person, place, or article, the effect of which was to prevent any native meddling with it. Going on shore to set up the observatory, permission was requested to place it in a certain field, upon which the priests immediately fixed their wands along the walls enclosing it, tabooing it—according to their phrase—after which not a man or woman among them dared to enter without express command or permission. Canoes did not venture even to land on the beach near it. The freedom from impertinent curiosity and thieving thus secured was invaluable for scientific observers. This taboo was not confined to the Sandwich Islands. Tongataboo, the principal of the Friendly Islands, owes its name to the practice: it is the residence of the king, and the name literally means Tonga—that is, the name of the island—taboo, set aside, or consecrated, as the king's own island.

The friendship of the two chiefs already spoken of proved also a highly convenient one to our people, owing to the good will of the pair, and the great power possessed by them over their inferior countrymen, whose love of seeing everything that was going on was sometimes not a little troublesome to those whom they visited. One day the decks of the "Resolution" so swarmed with natives that there was absolutely no getting on with ship's duty; one of these chiefs was therefore requested to lend a helping hand towards clearing them away. At a word from him they jumped overboard, all but one man, who, not being as prompt as the others, was immediately clutched in the chief's strong arms, and pitched into the sea after the rest. This chief was a fine fellow: athletic, well made, carrying his tall figure with an easy grace, whilst his handsome, expressive countenance was lighted up by dark, lively eyes. There were various ranks among the chiefs, and those of high grades could be brisk enough in their treatment of those in a lower position. This same fine-looking fellow, on one occasion, laid hold of an inferior chief, and nearly dragged him out of the cabin by the hair of his head, because, forsooth, my lord found him seated at dinner with Captain Cook—a distinction to which the great man thought he was not entitled, especially when the seat was wanted by himself. With the utmost wish to be civil to everybody, those around were obliged to let Pareea have his own way; at least, so far as to seat his victim on the floor, whilst he himself took the place at table thus compulsorily left empty.

On the 24th of January considerable surprise was felt on finding that no canoes came off as usual; nor were any natives to be seen on the beach. It was presently made known that the entire bay was tabooed, owing to the arrival of the king of Hawaii, who in the afternoon put off from the shore, and visited the ships privately. Next day a state visit was paid by him. In a large canoe were the king, Terreeoboo, and his chiefs, fully armed, and dressed in those beautiful feathered cloaks and caps which have been mentioned before. Another canoe contained priests (the priests had from the first been particularly kind and attentive to our people), with monstrous wicker-work idols of hideous fashion, having pearl-oysters for eyes. A third was filled with pigs and vegetables. These canoes paddled about for a time, the priests chanting; and, after parading round the ship, made for that part of the shore where the observatory was set up. The guard there was immediately turned out to receive his majesty; and Captain Cook, putting off from the "Resolution" to meet him, came ashore almost at the same instant. Both were marshalled to the tent, where the king, in a dignified manner, threw his own cloak around the captain, put a feathered cap on his head, and a curious fan in his hand, spreading at his feet, also, several other exceedingly rich cloaks. A profuse supply of provisions was then brought forward; and the interview ended by the exchange of names between Cook and the little old king. In returning, the captain took Terreeoboo, and a boat-load of his chiefs, on board the "Resolution," where they were received with all the attention due to their rank: the king himself getting a linen shirt, and the captain's own sword girded around his waist.

Everything seemed pleasant and prosperous, except for the annoyance—to which our people were pretty well accustomed by this time—of the islanders' thievish propensities. Of course these poor ignorant beings stole—much as a dog or cat steals. But they were excessively adroit and cultivated in the art of stealing. One day some ready-handed gentry were discovered beneath the ship, drawing out the nails that fastened her sheathing: a neat bit of work accomplished with the help of a very ingenious tool, designed for the purpose. This was rather more than could be borne; but as firing small shot only led them to dive, with the utmost unconcern, under the ship's bottom, it was thought desirable to give one of the offenders, luckily laid hold of, a flogging on her deck.

A little later on, there was a death on board the "Resolution:" that of an old sailor, so attached to his captain, with whom he had served before, that he had left his snug berth in Greenwich Hospital to join him in this expedition—the last to both of them. At the king's friendly request, William Watman, "able seaman" (humble yet honourable rank), was laid to rest among the great and honourable of this newly-discovered island, within the sacred enclosure of their morai. Whilst the burial service was being read over the poor fellow, the priests were silent, respectful spectators of the ceremony: then, when those around began to fill up the grave, they advanced, and showed their regard for the dead and his living companions, after their own notion of what was kind and reverential, throwing into it that unfailing pig (was it a sacred animal, as well as almost the only one for food?) together with cocoa-nuts and plantains. And for three nights after they continued around it their long ceremonies of sacrifice, chants, and prayers.

Still, notwithstanding their kind hospitality, the king and his chiefs seemed anxious that their visitants should be gone. The reason of their coming had been divined by them already: it was, that they were short of food in their own country; and, seeing that by this time they were unmistakeably fattened up on good baked pig, pudding, and vegetables—of which their excellent appetites threatened to produce some scarcity—it was not understood why they should remain any longer. To quiet these misgivings, the great people of Hawaii were told that the ships were to sail in a day or two; and on this announcement, proclamation was made that all should bring in pigs and vegetables for the Orono on his departure.

On the 3rd of February, in obedience to a summons from the king, Captain Cook and Lieutenant King went on shore. They found him amid an amazing quantity of articles of all kinds—eatables, wearables, and ornaments—including a large drove of pigs, which were grunting aloud near at hand, and many hatchets and other iron-ware, got from the ship; the whole being, as they were told, tribute to the king from his subjects. The iron, red feathers, and cloth were all spread out before the delighted monarch; and after having set aside a due proportion of them for himself, the remainder of the cloth, with the vast stock of pigs and vegetables, was munificently presented to the captain and his lieutenant. It was the largest gift of the kind they had ever received in these Southern Pacific Islands. Some of the pigs were destined to the salting-tub, for sea-store, while the smaller ones—there were thirty of these—and vegetables, made savoury fare for the crews of the two vessels. How could mischief be expected from such kindly savages? Further, Lieutenant King, who had charge of the observatory and shore party, had made himself so well liked by the priests and others with whom he had to do, that when the ships were on the point of sailing he was strongly urged (with many assurances of its being to his advantage) to remain behind. To give to mere savages, however kindly, a point-blank refusal of that upon which they had set their minds, was an awkward matter; so Mr. King tried to get out of it by telling his urgent friends that the Orono would not consent to his remaining with them. But for this difficulty they were quite prepared: suggesting to him that he should hide in the mountains until the ships had taken their departure from the bay. To this was replied that the captain would never sail without his lieutenant; and then the king frankly asked Cook to leave his son—as they supposed the lieutenant to be—with them. It was an embarrassing piece of work, but Cook did the best he could, by saying that he could not spare Mr. King at present: as he intended returning to the islands in the course of the next year, he would then see what could be done to oblige them in this matter.

On the 4th of February the ships sailed out of the bay, accompanied by a little fleet of canoes, and having received another liberal gift of provisions from the king of the islands. Their design was to make more exploration of the group before starting for the north; but squalls beset them. Old Koah, who out of compliment had changed his name to Brittanee, and shipped himself as pilot, proved bad at his new trade; and matters turned out so, that by the 10th the vessels were compelled to return to the anchorage which they had only a few days before left.

Oh, if they had only not had to return to that fatal spot, all might have been well!

But Cook's work was done : a hard and good day's work in his time. One grudges, though, that such a name should be erased from the list of the living by mere savages.

Before returning to this treacherous haven, Cook had, with the humanity habitual to him, stopped the ship's way to take up a couple of wretched islanders who, having been driven off the coast in their canoe by the storm, were so exhausted with battling against it, that they could scarcely have got on deck had not one of the natives still on board the " Resolution," seeing their condition, jumped down and made their litt'e skiff fast to the rope thrown out to them. Three others had already been saved by Mr. Bligh in the pinnace.

CHAPTER XVII.

KARAKAKOOA BAY.—NATIVES TROUBLESOME.—ATTACK ON THE
ENGLISH.—CAPTAIN COOK SLAIN.

THE ships were at their old moorings again in Karakakooa Bay on the 10th of February; and as the foremast of the "Resolution" was injured, not only by the storm but by the wear and tear of her long voyages in alternately hot and frozen climates, it had to be got out, and sent on shore for repairs. The priests, as before, tabooed the spot where it and the carpenters were placed, by this means freeing the workmen from all interference of native curiosity, and their valuable tools from the depredations of light-fingered lookers-on. So far, all was still friendly as ever; but other appearances caused our people to think that their return to the bay was not altogether liked at Hawaii. Why it should not they could not conjecture, but the impression upon their minds was strong. Next morning, however, things brightened; for the king, whose absence had been supposed to account for the change, returned to the bay, came on board the "Resolution," with all the friendliness of his former manner; the natives, after this, resumed their intercourse with the ships, and it was supposed all was right again.

So the cloud seemed to blow away. But it was only to gather more thickly and darkly. On the 13th, an officer who commanded the watering party sent from the "Discovery," reported that some chiefs had driven away the natives engaged to help in rolling the casks down to the shore: a bit of work which, as has been mentioned, the people of the numerous islands already visited had been glad to undertake for trifling payment of nails, beads, or such little things. As he expressed a fear that they intended making themselves still more troublesome, a marine, with side-arms only, was sent back with him, in hopes of overawing the malcontents. But, spite of the redcoat, the turbulent islanders waxed ruder, and, beginning to arm with stones, it was thought discreet to send others to the spot—an officer, and marine with loaded musket. This settled affairs for the time; and Captain Cook, to whom the whole circumstances were made known, gave orders that if the natives made any attack upon his people, ball cartridges should be used in return, instead of the ordinary small shot.

It was not long before a peppering of musketry, after a canoe rapidly paddling ashore from the "Discovery," announced some mischief in that direction. The old story —thieving; and, in ignorance of the stolen goods having been got back again, chase was given by Cook, another officer, and a marine, on shore; until, at almost nightfall, finding it had carried them some distance from the tents, the pursuers deemed it prudent to abandon their game and return to their station.

It seemed as if a fatality hung over our people during

this most unfortunate second visit to the island; for, on returning, chafed and baffled, from this fruitless pursuit of the thieves, it was found that a worse difficulty had sprung up. The officer, who had already recovered the stolen articles, on returning, saw a canoe drawn up on the beach; and it occurred to his wise head to take possession of it, by way of retaliation or punishment. And more was the pity; for the canoe belonged to their old friend Pareea, who, coming up at the instant from on board the "Discovery," warmly resented the seizure, and, in the scuffle that followed, got such a blow on the head with an oar as felled him. The lookers-on immediately avenged this with a shower of stones; and would, further, have destroyed the pinnace—whose crew were obliged to swim out to a distant rock for shelter—had not the chief's hard head fortunately not been much the worse for the heavy knock it had received, and for which he apparently bore no malice, for he instantly exerted himself to drive away the wreckers, and then made signs to the boat's crew, clinging like seafowl to their rock of refuge, to come back and take their craft off. He even so far put himself out of the way as to paddle after them in his canoe, with some trifling articles stolen from the pinnace, which he had been at the pains to recover, asking, as it seemed with genuine feeling, whether the Orono—Cook's native title—would kill him in consequence of what had happened, and whether he would be allowed to come on board next day. He was assured that he would be welcome, on which satisfactory communication he joined noses with the officers (Hawaiian hand-shaking), and went his way.

DISTURBANCES.

Captain Cook was very uneasy at what had taken place. To serious disturbances like these he was not used, and he feared they would drive him to what he had always anxiously avoided—the using harsh measures towards the savages with whom he had to deal; for he was well aware it would never do to allow such to suppose that he was afraid of them. Near two hundred British lives were entrusted to his keeping; and the charge was weighty enough to press severely on a high-souled man, with a conscience, like Cook. It was too late to take any measures for that night, save the one of sending ashore all the natives on board, which was done at once: a clean sweep was made of the whole lot. In the course of this night, however, a boat belonging to the "Discovery" was cut from the buoy to which it was moored; and, on information of its loss, Cook at once ordered an armed party of marines ashore, going with them himself with his double-barrelled gun; one barrel loaded with small shot—according to his humane custom—the other with ball, in case of serious work. His intention was to follow his usual plan in such troublesome circumstances: get either the king, or some of the chiefs, into his power, and retain his prize until the boat was given up. It had not unfrequently been found that native chiefs, if not actually thieves themselves, employed or countenanced their inferiors in thieving, all the time being amiably willing, nay, anxious, to have them punished if found out, whilst themselves sneaked off unhurt; so that endangering their own precious persons was found the only effectual means of getting redress in such cases. The boats of both ships were all ordered out, and stationed so as to prevent any canoes leaving the bay; indeed, they were to seize and destroy them, if milder methods did not serve for the recovery of the cutter. It would have been risking British lives to let that boat go. The captain's last orders, before going ashore on this sad errand, were that Mr. King, the lieutenant on shore, should make the natives understand that no harm was meant them; while, at the same time, he was to keep a good watch against surprise from their quarter.

After this he took boat with Lieutenant Phillips, of the marines, and nine of his men; and, on reaching the shore, at once marched them to the village where the king lived; the people, as usual, falling down before him, and bringing the accustomed offerings. He speedily hunted up the king (whose manner was convincing that he had no hand in the theft), and his two sons, who had been the captain's frequent visitors on board the "Resolution;" and, at his request, they willingly consented to return with him to the ship. The two young men were already in the pinnace, to which their father was advancing, apparently with all good faith, when his wife followed him, and, with tears, entreated him not to go on board. Her prayers and efforts were seconded pretty roughly by two chiefs, who, laying hold of him, forced him to sit down on the beach, where he remained, evidently frightened almost out of his senses, between their forcible dealings with him, and Captain Cook's urgent persuasions that he should accompany him to the ship. Things began to look bad. Persuasions on one side, force and violence on the other: it was no wonder that the feeble old king fell under the power of the latter;

and Cook, seeing from the threatening appearance of all around that, if he also resorted to force, numbers of the savages, now gathered in thousands about him, might lose their lives, gave it up, and turned slowly to the beach to re-embark.

In sudden and murderous tumults the order of events is never clear. Even eye-witnesses will rarely agree in their account of them; so that we must do the best we can with what is told us about this melancholy affair. It seems that the boats stationed to guard the bay had fired on some escaping canoes, and in doing so killed a chief; news of which unfortunately arrived just as Cook—for peace sake, giving up his design for the recovery of the cutter, and teaching the islanders that he was not to be insulted with impunity—was proceeding to the boat, in order to return to his ship. Under this fresh irritation the natives began to arm, and put on their war-mats; and one of them, carrying an iron spike, or dagger, which he brandished defiantly, threatened the captain with a stone, which, after the manner of these people, was another of his weapons—and no trifling one either, thrown with the full force of brawny savage arms. Cook in vain tried to make the man be quiet; and at last, tired out with his insolent menaces, gave him the contents of the barrel loaded with small shot, which, alas! against the fellow's thick war-mat, were no better than so many hail-stones. Then stones were thrown; an attempt was made to stab the marine officer, which failing, was returned by him with a hearty blow from his clubbed musket; and, driven to it at last, Cook (as a fellow sneaking behind a double canoe aimed a spear at him) gave them his second barrel, loaded with ball, and killed one of the assailants. Then came more stone-throwing, answered by a volley from the marines (four of whom were speedily destroyed by the savages) and boats; and before our people had time to load again, it was all over with them, in this deadly hand-to-hand scuffle.

The captain stood at the water's edge, signalling the boats to stop firing, and pull in to take the marines and himself on board; but again there was confusion and mistake. The lieutenant commanding one of the boats, apparently misapprehending what was wanted, put his boat further off, and so threw the picking up of the marines—some of them wounded, and struggling in the water—entirely on the pinnace; the unfortunate commander being left alone on the rock, where he was seen with one hand behind his head to shield it from the shower of stones, the other still holding his musket, endeavouring to make his way to the pinnace, which had been brought as near to as the master dared, for fear of grounding her.

It is hard for one who has followed Cook's career, even through these three voyages only, to describe what now took place. So soon as his back was turned to them, the natives plucked up courage to attack him; one, as though frightened at what he was doing, gave him, with a club, so stunning a blow on the back of the head, as sent him down on one hand and knee, dropping his musket in the fall. Before he could recover himself another stabbed him in the back of the neck: again he dropped in knee-deep water, where the wretches crowded upon him to keep him under; but his struggles brought his head up, looking earnestly towards the pinnace, which, though not more than a few yards off, somehow could do nothing to save him whose whole care had been for the safety of them and their comrades. To think any one, even in that crowded, embarrassed boat, could see that look, and not strain every muscle to rescue him!

Again the savages got him under, in deeper water; and in his last death struggle, writhing himself from their murderous gripe, he endeavoured to cling to the rock, when,—one more blow, and there was an end. His lifeless body, dragged upon the beach, was pierced over and over again by the daggers of these pitiless beings, who seemed to take a ferocious delight in inflicting their now harmless strokes on him who had so earnestly striven to be the friend and benefactor of their race, and had now lost his life that theirs might be spared.

There must have been a terrible want of judgment or zeal—or we know not what—when such a man as Cook could thus be left to be deliberately murdered, within a few yards of two good-sized boats, under naval discipline; and complaints enough were made by some of the indignant survivors. "Some one had blundered;" but it was a terrible mistake, that there was no remedying. After the fall of their commander, a smart fire was still kept up from the boats, under cover of which the survivors made their escape: one marine, a bad swimmer, being rescued by his already wounded officer, who jumped into the water after him, and, spite of such a blow on the head with a stone as sent him to the bottom, gripped the man by his hair and got him safe on board. This incessant musketry, together with more shot from the four-pounders of the "Resolution," at length forced the rabble to fall back.

It was not until after strange delay that Cook's remains —remains literally, for his poor body had been hacked in pieces and distributed among his slayers, so that only a portion of it could be recovered—were got back, and committed with reverent sorrow to the deep: the guns pealing over the bright waters in which sank the bones of one of England's greatest, truest sons, as they would have done over his grave.

Captain Clerke, Cook's brother officer, and his successor in command of the expedition, was in weak health at the time—he died long before the ships got home again—and that doubtless rendered him scarcely fit to deal properly with the difficulties arising out of this terrible mischance.

By demand of the English, the bay was tabooed when they were about to perform the last rites for their dead leader; so that solemn silence rested around, unbroken even by the plash of the tiniest canoe. Twenty-four hours of this enforced tribute to his memory satisfied them, and the islanders were then permitted to bring the ordinary supplies and to pay their accustomed visits: all but one rascally, hypocritical old priest, who, on presenting himself as usual, was briskly sent about his business.

Cook was in the prime of life, only fifty-one, when he was thus barbarously slain at Hawaii. But his work was done: a hard and good day's work in his time, from the date when, twenty years before, he had piloted our boats to attack the French, with whom we were at war, in Canada, to that in which, still labouring in the cause of science and humanity, both largely benefited by him, he drew his last breath amid a throng of murderers. Such a fate, for such a man, is heart-breaking.

What this great Englishman did for his own country and the world outside it, in the last ten years of his life, was enough for many a lifetime, and may be briefly summed up. He not only sailed three times round the world—a much more arduous undertaking a century ago than it is now, when steam shortens both space and time—but in those three long, trying voyages, besides mapping the seas, and finding out almost numberless small islands, he discovered the important cluster of the Society Islands, the Sandwich Islands, the Friendly Isles, and some of the New Hebrides: New Caledonia, one of the latter, is the largest island except one in the Southern Pacific Ocean. He added greatly to our knowledge of New Holland—our modern New South Wales,—New Zealand, and Van Diemen's Land, as well as other countries and islands previously little known. His researches towards the South Pole proved that there was not, as had long been believed, a continent in that region of icy waters, or, if there were one that had eluded him, that it was so completely blocked within the frozen zone as to be useless to man. And though he, as well as a host of others, failed to find that North West or North East Passage which we now know of simply as a subject of curiosity—it is useless—his northern explorations contributed greatly to the extent and accuracy of our acquaintance with that part of the world and its people.

In the course of this work he taught both ourselves and

all Europeans how to manage these long sojourns at sea, with less wretchedness and loss of life to those engaged in them than had been known before his time; whilst among the numerous and important islands first found or more clearly made out by him, there was not one that, to the utmost of his power, he did not seek to leave the better for his finding or examining it.

It is always interesting to know something of the personal appearance of great men. Cook is described as spare and tall—more than six feet high, with small head, quick, piercing eyes, prominent eyebrows, face full of expression, but with somewhat of austerity in the look—a face to be studied, and then admired. His hair was brown, tied behind in what was called a *queue*, after the strange fashion of the day. In constitution he was strong and untiring, fitted for all the hardships that fell to his lot. His manners, as might be supposed, were plain and simple.

For a firm, quiet, modest, manly, heroic character like his, we could find no better epitaph than one placed over the tomb of another of our English, of recent times, whose quiet heroism was proved during the Indian mutiny: it needs but a change of name:—

"Here lies James Cook, who tried to do his duty."

But, alas! the great discoverer lies, we know not where, in the depths of the Southern Pacific.

CHAPTER XVIII.

Leave Karakakooa Bay.—Kamschatka.—Harbour of St. Peter and St. Paul.—Russian Hospitality.—Dog Sledges.—The Capital of Kamschatka.—Generous Kindness of the Russian Governor.—Try again for the North West Passage, and again Foiled.—Walrus and White Bears.—Death of Captain Clerke.—Return to St. Peter and St. Paul.—Bear-hunting.—China.—Home.

THE story of Cook's exploring expedition, after Cook himself was sunk in his ocean grave, does not seem to possess much interest; but we must briefly sketch it, because it formed a portion of his plan, which it fell to Captain Clerke, as his successor in command, to carry out. As head of the expedition, Clerke now removed to the "Resolution," giving his own ship, the "Discovery," to Cook's late first lieutenant, Mr. Gore. There seemed, as we have said, a strange heedlessness about their great commander, both at the time of his cruel slaughter and immediately after his death. Vengeance for that death was, however, at last taken; and, perhaps, more heavily than if it had more speedily followed the crime; for the seamen had been almost driven mad by the insolence of the natives, one of whom, after slinging stones at them, triumphantly waved Captain Cook's hat over his head, a sight that put the discipline of British sailors to an almost too severe trial.

The fatal bay was left on the 22nd of February, but the ship continued for a while among the islands. At Atooi, one of their first discoveries, they anchored for a supply of water and other needful things. But they did not get on so comfortably as on their former visit, partly owing to misconduct of the crew at the time, of a kind that Cook had always done his utmost to prevent: partly, as we may well believe, that the master-mind that had hitherto controlled all with so much firmness, wisdom, and kindness, was now withdrawn from them. The natives became troublesome, mischievous, full of what, for their provoking nature, might be called monkey-tricks. To begin with, one of them got a thrust with a bayonet, whilst the marines were with some difficulty keeping the watering party from pressure; and as he did not like it, he resented it by trying to wrench the musket out of the man's hand, and, when foiled in that, coming full butt, spear in one hand, dagger in the other, to avenge himself upon his enemy. Then, with the greed of the Nootka Sound people, who were determined to be paid for everything had from their dreary shores, even wood and water, a large hatchet was demanded in return for each caskful: a demand which, if complied with, would have converted water into a very expensive luxury indeed. When refused this, they either would not allow the casks to be rolled down to the boats, or, pretending to help in doing it, would give them a sly twist on one side, so that they went in the wrong direction; whilst all the time, amid shouts and laughter, the sailors' hats were filched off their heads, their heels tripped up, or their clothes jerked so as to pull them backwards. Never were such irritating monkey-tricks played off on a party of busy men, all seriously engaged on important business. One longs for some one to have taken a good horsewhip to the whole lot of them. That common soldiers and sailors should stand this sort of nonsense was almost more than could be expected; but stand it they did, with tact as well as forbearance, taking it, as long as possible, as though it were in jest; and when that could no longer be done, meeting their tormentors boldly and firmly. But, with all this care and forbearance, they did not get the water-casks off without having to use their muskets, which, to the great regret of the officer on duty, sharply hit one of the natives.

While all this was going on, Captain Clerke was in a terrible state of anxiety about his people. He had a party of islanders on board at the time, filling his ears with a doleful narrative of how their chiefs had quarrelled over the goats left by Cook, and in the squabble, instead of damaging themselves, which would have been no great matter, had killed the poor goats; a narrative that his anxious condition, and small acquaintance with their language, translated into one of Captain Cook's death at Hawaii. And, seeing flashes of musketry in the distance, he could only conclude that the tragedy was to be repeated here.

These most disastrous islands were finally left on the 15th of March, and from them a tolerably straight course north-west was taken to the coast of Kamschatka, where, in case of separation, the harbour of St. Peter and St. Paul was to be their place of meeting before trying again for that passage—north-east or north-west, according to the point whence people sought it—between the northern continents.

The chief incidents of this run were the troublesome leakage of the "Resolution," which occasioned much labour and anxiety; and the seeking for certain islands, reported by former navigators, which, as they could not now be found, were conjectured to be imaginary.

Mistakes will happen. We all know the story of the captain who spent some days sailing round what turned out to be a speck of dirt upon his chart, but which he had taken for an island, laid down in that latitude.

By the 18th of the month the cold of the northern regions into which they had made their way was severely felt; and the sailors, who, in the pleasant warmth of the south, had kicked their furs and warm dresses about the decks, hither and thither—anywhere out of the way—were now indebted to the providence of their officers, who had had the despised garments picked up and put carefully aside until wanted. With the ship so crusted over with ice, that the shrouds were more than twice as big again, warm clothing was to be desired.

April 28th the harbour was sighted, and glances were eagerly directed towards it in search of the town of Petropaulowska—that is Russ for the town of Peter and

Paul. The bay was swept from end to end by their glasses for what was expected to be a place of considerable strength and importance. At last, on a long spit of land, some miserable log-houses and huts were descried, and as no other signs of habitation could be made out, even by the sharpest eyes, they were compelled to conclude that this beggarly affair was indeed what they sought.

Bad as it was, it had, however, to be got at; and in attempting to land, Mr. King fell through the ice; so that his appearance was not particularly imposing when, after many difficulties of various kinds, he at length came in presence of the Russian commander, who, cane in hand, at the head of his little garrison of thirty men, came marching out to meet his visitors. As neither understood a word said by the other, it was in vain that Mr. King tried to convince the good Russian that the party were English. Mr. Ismyloff's letters were, however, handed to him (had their contents been known there would scarcely have been any hurry about this), and then, wheeling round his band, with cautious steps and slow, he conducted the new-comers to the town, halting and manœuvring his men from time to time, in order to impress the little party of foreigners with the extreme military character of the force under his command. The performance was very amusing, even to Mr. King, wet through, and shivering from his exceedingly cold bath on the frozen coast of Kamschatka.

On arriving at the commander's house, it was found that due military precautions had been taken against the strangers in the bay, whose hostile landing had been prepared for by placing a couple of small field-pieces at his door. Ammunition, and even lighted matches, were at hand, for there were no percussion-locks to cannon in those days; a piece of slightly-twisted, saltpetred hemp, which burned slowly, supplied their place.

But though prepared for war—guards were also posted about the house, after the dangerous guests had entered it—the Russian received our friends with much civility. Nay, after one letter had been opened, and the other sent off to the governor at some distance, their host got over his fright, and was all attention and real kindness: giving freezing and dripping Mr. King a suit of dry clothes in exchange for his wet ones, and setting down the party to as good a dinner as could be served at such short notice. Soup there was none. But how could that be regretted when there was the appetising substitute of slices of cold beef, with hot water poured over them? After this came a large roasted bird, name unknown; but as it was very good, that was of no consequence; then two dishes of fish, followed by that marvellous bird again, or rather, what had been left of it, withdrawn awhile to make its re-appearance in the disguise of little pies, sweet and savoury. It was well said, that the Russians were good cooks; and without doubt the commander's wife (he was only a sergeant, yet showed himself a gentleman), who brought in several of the dishes, had had a hand in the preparing them. Quass, a coarse Russian spirit, was produced to "wash down" the hospitable entertainment, and was the worst part of it. Bows and friendly gesticulations made up the conversation at table; but when business came on afterwards it was not without extreme difficulty that an understanding between the parties was come to, to the effect that neither provisions nor naval stores were to be had at Petropaulowska: at head-quarters, whither one of the letters had been sent, they were in abundance; but, until permission was had from thence, neither the sergeant, nor anybody else in this long-named town, dared even go on board the ships.

The sergeant, however, did what he could. Sledges, each drawn by five dogs, were brought out to take the English to their vessels; a drive that delighted the sailors, more especially when they saw that a couple of boat-hooks, which they had with them, had a sledge all to themselves. Wrapped up in his host's clothes, for his own were still too wet to put on, Mr. King took his party back again, all being of opinion that sledging over broken ice was much easier than walking over it.

Our English little knew what a fright this visit of theirs gave, not only the sergeant, but the whole population of the town: for it seems that friendly Mr. Ismyloff, of Oonalashka, had thought proper in his letter to describe their ships as two small trading vessels, and themselves as probably pirates; which bit of maliciousness (perhaps sheer ignorance) had excessively puzzled and alarmed their really good friends the Russians. Two men-of-war, which it was taken for granted were French, introduced in such terms, were quite enough to lead to the fear of some violent attack on this far-distant and very cold possession of theirs; and the inhabitants would, in very terror, have fled into the interior, had they not been prevented by the governor. Confidence being restored, unbounded hospitality and good will were shown to our people, who had reason to feel deeply grateful to the subjects, in this part of the world, of their ally, the great Empress Catherine of Russia.

Stores and provisions, as has been said, were not to be had here, but from head-quarters. So Captain Gore, Mr. King, and a small party were despatched thither on the 7th of May, travelling in canoes, boats, and sledges, according to the nature of their route.

To these sledges the dogs were yoked, two and two, with one in front as leader, whose education for his duties was most careful, and begun in very early life, as, indeed, was that of his more humble companions. Careful training of these beasts was specially needed; for the reins, being fastened to the collar, instead of to the head of the animal, were not of much use in guiding him: as any one who has chanced to have a horse thus harnessed at a country inn well knows. In this case the voice of the driver, and his stick, served both to direct and control his steeds; the stick being struck into the snow so as to check, or even entirely stop the sledge: whilst it did duty as whip, being hurled with unerring aim at any offender in the team, and dexterously caught up again in passing, after fulfilling its mission of punishment. According to custom, the dogs were prepared for their long journey by a whole day's fast; and as, also according to custom, they were never fed on the road, it may be understood that they occasionally make a meal of their own trappings. Even to human beings, old leather is better than starvation. These beasts were something like the Pomeranian dog, only larger. They were generally of a light dun, or dirty cream colour; and the mode of training them for draught was, when they were young, to fasten them by strips of elastic leather to a stake, and then place their food at such a distance that to get it they were forced to pull and strain against their bonds. A habit of pulling against any weight at their heels was thus acquired, that turned to good account when harnessed to the sledge. It seems exceedingly like making a donkey go, by holding a bunch of carrots before its nose. During summer the dogs were turned out to find their own living. When the winter snow fell, they were sure to come home, where they were fed upon the bones and other refuse of salmon prepared for their masters' food.

Great skill was also required on the part of the drivers of these sledges. Mr. King's charioteer was a good-humoured but very clumsy fellow, who contrived to overturn his master almost every minute, to the great amusement of his companions, who were more fortunate in their conductors. It was the old story: "sport" to them, but bumps and bruises to the unlucky lieutenant.

Their first night during this expedition was spent gipsy-fashion; in a country which, not only from its latitude, but from its being exposed to sweeping winds laden with all the cold of a wide, uncultivated tract of land, was anything but well adapted to this kind of camping out, at least for Englishmen, unaccustomed as they generally are to such rough doings. The ground selected was first cleared of snow; then a tent was set up; but, bitter cold as it was, the fire had to be lighted at some distance from those who would have liked to huddle over the cheery blaze, because its thawing of the frozen earth upon which it was kindled, created around it an extensive hearth-place of puddle. Their Kamschadale attendants regaled themselves here on hot tea, for the providing of which they had with them tea-kettles : tea, two or three times a-day, being regarded by them as one of the necessaries of life.

The next evening some rest was had at the hut of one of the chief people of this part of the country, who gave them a good dinner of fish, game, and heath-berries to begin with, backed by so hearty a welcome as would have made worse fare go down well. As, after a thaw which had taken place, the ground was not hard enough for sledging, the good man beguiled their delay by, in the next place, giving his guests a supper as good as their dinner. In return for these hospitalities, he and his wife received generous presents from Captain Gore, and were also treated by him to hot punch. Then the travellers spread their bear-skins on the wooden benches of the hut, and got a comfortable nap before continuing their journey, late in the evening.

Head-quarters—that is, Bolcheretsk—were at length neared; and our travellers, who not, for long, having had occasion to think about appearance, had bundled themselves up for the journey in anything that came to hand, heedless that English, Indian, and Kamschadale tailors might all have had a hand in it, were a little alarmed on finding that they were expected to make something like a public entry into the capital. That they were ludicrous objects, had not occurred to them before; but it was a fact to which they now woke up so painfully that their only resource was a desperate attempt to stop, like John Gilpin's chaise, "three doors off:" sending a polite message to the governor not to trouble himself to come and meet them, for as soon as they had changed their dress they would wait upon him. His excellency was not, however, to be outdone in politeness; and so our unhappy friends were obliged to parade their harlequin costume before the eyes of all the "rank, beauty, and fashion" of Bolcheretsk, finding also, to their further mortification, that two years and a-half of savage life had rendered their manners almost as unpresentable as their clothes. In the course of that time the making of a bow had very nearly become a lost art. But the treatment they received in this remote and forlorn part of the world was hospitable and generous in the extreme; not only were substantial benefits showered upon them, but honours of the most unexpected kind were added: guards turned out with military promptitude as they passed to the house appointed for their residence, sentinels were posted at their door, and the like.

The governor would not even allow Captain Gore to pay for the ample ships' stores procured here; telling him, that nothing could more highly gratify the empress, his mistress, than to know that her dominions had been able to afford the least help or comfort to her good friends and allies, the English, especially to vessels engaged in such a service as that of the present expedition.

A very singular circumstance occurred whilst our people were at Bolcheretsk. Despatches were received by the governor, informing him that the Tschutski—the inhabi-

V

tants of that extreme eastern point of Asia visited by Captain Cook the year before—had voluntarily offered, what previously they could never be compelled to yield: namely, friendship and tribute to the Russians; by whom, as they said, they had been visited in two large boats, and so kindly treated that they had, at the time, made a league of peace with them, which was now desired to be drawn out into a formal treaty. The governor was puzzled, for he knew of no such visit from his nation. His English guests, however, furnished a key to the mystery: the simple Asiatics had, as it turned out, taken Cook for a Russian; so that his invariable goodness to all the uncivilised tribes with whom he came in contact, was on this occasion the means of procuring for the Russians what they could not have got for themselves. It was very pleasant for the English to know this, just when they were being laden with favours by those already, though unconsciously, indebted to them for so important an acquisition as the fealty of this Asiatic tribe.

On quitting Bolcheretsk, May 16th, fresh attentions awaited our people in this wilderness of a place. The whole of the garrison was drawn up on one hand, all the men of the town, in their holiday dress, on the other; and the moment Captain Gore and his companions made their appearance, these all united in a melancholy chant, according to the custom of Kamschatka on parting with friends. Thus, and headed by a military band, they proceeded to the governor's house, where they were received by his wife, and other ladies, magnificently clad in silks and furs; who, after offering refreshments, joined the procession in its plaintive song, and so conducted our friends to their boats, into which they were glad to get with all speed, to conceal the feelings excited by this affecting leave-taking. On putting off, three good, honest cheers from those on shore bade them God-speed on their journey.

In addition to other acts of kindness on the part of these friendly people, a good Russian priest, whose house was sixteen miles from the harbour, every day sent poor Captain Clerke, who was dying of consumption, bread, milk, butter, and poultry; and the captain, happily, had it in his power to make an invaluable return for this and other humane and generous attentions received by him and his people, by placing the hospital of Petropaulowska, where sea-scurvy was raging, under the care of the ship's surgeons. Their experienced treatment, together with the ample supplies of sour-krout and wort sent on shore by the captain, soon produced so great a change in the health both of soldiers and the people of the place, as utterly to astonish Gore and his party after their fortnight's absence. This must have afforded real pleasure to the captain and all under his command.

The harbour was left on the 16th of June; a volcanic mountain, near thirty miles off, having the day before treated them to an eruption, which covered the ships almost an inch thick with dust, that looked like emery powder, followed by showers of cinders, from the size of a pea to that of a hazel-nut, and some small stones. A mountain of such capabilities was best thirty miles out of the way.

Behring's Strait was again entered; and, on the 6th of July, at ten o'clock of a clear night, our voyagers had before them the remarkable spectacle of the two extreme points of Asia and America: Cape East, rearing its high, round, snow-capped head, and Cape Prince of Wales, distinguished by its neighbouring spiky hill, with the two small snowy islands of St. Diomede lying between them.

Captain Clerke's attempts, made in various directions, to push to the extreme north, were as fruitless as those of his predecessor had been, being baffled by the same obstacle, ice, ice, ice—impenetrable ice. Nay, they were rather more so, as on the 27th of July, when he was compelled to give up the search for that northern passage, he had not reached quite so high a latitude as had been attained by Cook.

Some walrus were got in these regions, as before. One mother-walrus, whose young one had been killed, attacked the boat with such fury that she sent her tusks right through the bottom of it. White bears, of which they secured a couple, though fishy in flavour, were found very superior diet to walrus.

After three years' absence from home, the order to "'bout-ship" was joyfully received by every one on board. On this northward course, by the 17th of August, the invalid, unable to leave his bed, was obliged to commit his duties as commander to the first lieutenant, Mr. King; in less than a week after, he was dead, having thus been in harness literally to the last. There is something grand and heroic in a man's thus calmly struggling on until his life and his charge are laid down almost at the same moment; and such heroism may be, and is, practised in the quietest, least distinguished posts that fall to the lot of

POLAR BEAR.

human beings. Heroism must be in the soul: it does not depend upon circumstance.

Young as Captain Clerke was—he was only thirty-seven –this was his fourth voyage round the world. Returning to their hospitable friends of the harbour of St. Peter and St. Paul, his comrades laid to rest the worn-out body—worn out in the honourable toil of his profession—according to his wish, in mother earth, beneath a tree which marked out the site of an intended church that would afterwards enclose his grave: the whole Russian population joining in the last token of respect to his memory.

A change of officers took place in consequence of his death: Captain Gore, from the "Discovery," taking the "Resolution," and its first lieutenant, Mr. King, being appointed to the command of the former. The juniors had also their changes and promotions.

Repairing the ships—sorely battered by their encounters with arctic ice—brewing spruce beer, spearing and salting salmon, boiling down sea-horse blubber for oil (to supply the place of candles), with an occasional bear-hunt, pretty well filled up the time during this stay in the harbour. The bear was an important animal in Kamschatka, as, by the admission of the natives themselves, they were indebted to it, not only for all their medical skill (acquired by notice of the various herbs used by it for its hurts and ailments), but also for their sole instruction in the art of dancing; all the steps and movements of that accomplishment being strictly copied from those of this unwieldy beast. "If the bear praises my dancing," says the monkey in the fable, "I must dance ill." So we may imagine what a Kamschadale dance was like

The first bear-hunts in which our English took a part, were disappointing in their results: on one occasion there were too many persons in chase, on another the weather was against them. But a third, taken perhaps under abler generalship—that of the clerk of the parish, known as a mighty hunter—as well as during more suitable weather, turned out better. Arriving by sundown at one of the large lakes of the district, the hunters were directed to hide among the tall grass and brushwood on its margin. Crouched there, they soon had the satisfaction of hearing the brutes growling around them; and presently, in the clear moonlight, one was descried running in the direction of their hiding-place. When within sixteen yards, three well-aimed shots greeted its advance, hitting it so severely that, with horrible roars and growls, it turned short, and dragging itself up the bank, made for the covert of some bushes. As the roaring continued to be heard from this thicket, the hunters were convinced that they had "done" for their prey, though it was not safe to go in at once and "bag it." Discretion is the better part of valour; so they waited patiently until next morning, when they found their spoil, a huge she-bear, dead enough.

The "stalking" of these huge brutes is a dangerous sport; for if the first discharge of fire-arms does not kill, an impetuous rush on the assailants is made in return, which, unless cleverly received on the points of their spears, is pretty certain to prove fatal to some of the party.

The notion in the country was that during winter the bear subsists on sucking his paws; and that being but slender diet, he was doubly furious when spring came,

ALBATROSS.

and, therefore, more dangerous to be attacked at that season. The she-bear with her young one by her side was the most formidable; for if the cub were slain, her rage knew no bounds,—there was scarce any escaping it so that the hunter's only safe plan was to shoot the mother, when, if successful, the poor little one, still clinging to its dam, was an easy capture.

The bear, in spite of all these perils, was a prize worth contending for: his warm furry skin being useful for bedding and clothing, and his meat being reckoned so good as not to need the sauce requisite for rendering palatable some of the extreme northern dishes—that is, hunger. The bears seen on this occasion were all of a dull brown colour.

Whilst still at St. Peter and St. Paul, our voyagers had the annoyance of finding that their excellent friend the sergeant had, for some reason or other, fallen into disgrace with his superiors. Nay, the worthy man had had his own cane, or somebody else's, laid on his back, to the great distress of the English, who were not accustomed to the degrading severities of continental armies of that date. They had the satisfaction, however, of soon seeing the good fellow reinstated in the command which he had so well filled; while the new governor, who did him this justice, was highly displeased with the officer who had, without cause, subjected the sergeant to punishment. For another excellent friend of theirs, an old private soldier, they had also the pleasure of obtaining promotion to the rank of corporal: a grade of more dignity in the Russian service than in our own, and one which made the old man perfectly happy.

All being ready for sailing, plans for the future had to be decided upon; and after consultation with the officers, it was agreed that, considering the worn condition of the ships, their sails, and rigging, the only thing that could safely be done was to make for and survey the coast of Japan, examine the islands lying north of it, then sail for China, and so home. This course was therefore the one adopted; the snug little harbour of St. Peter and St. Paul, with its friendly people, being left on the 9th of October. But severe storms, that split their crazy, worn-out sails, and snapped their inadequate and rotted cordage, interfered with part of this purpose, by driving the ships from the dangerous coast of Japan: dangerous alike from natural obstacles, and from the obstinate determination of its people to have nothing to do with outsiders. In those days, and until almost modern times, even shipwrecked mariners had better have been contending with the stormiest waves, than have been cast on that most barbarous strand. So our voyagers reluctantly put up their helm, and bore away for rather less hazardous and inhospitable shores.

Rough weather continued to attend them. On the 13th of November, steering south-west in a violent gale, their advance southward was marked by the appearance of dolphins, flying-fish, and their old friend the swift, wide-winged albatross, "riding upon the storm," according to its wont, with all the graceful ease of its vast strength. On this occasion it escaped the degradation of being consigned to the stew-pan.

By the 4th of December, having carried out all the

practicable portions of their original plan, the two ships were safely moored in Chinese waters, guided therein by one of a couple of squabbling native pilots, who, brought on board by the signal for one, had a mind, apparently, to take forcible possession of the "Resolution;" the feud between them being finally healed by their agreeing to divide the fee for pilotage.

The Chinamen were sharp traders, and yet so ready and profitable a sale was met with among them for the worn furs—now considered useless—of our men; furs, some of them in the first instance got second-hand from their uncivilised owners, and then knocked about on ship-board, used as bed-clothes, or anything else—as rather to tempt some of the crew to return north for more skins, and make their fortunes as fur-traders. Indeed, as at this time two of the men were reported "missing, without leave," and a six-oared cutter was, at precisely the same moment, reported missing, it could only be concluded that they had gone off in its company, finding the fur-trading temptation irresistible. What became of the poor wretches nobody knew.

Notwithstanding that the Chinese are proverbially provoking to deal with, our voyagers, on the whole, got on better with them than might have been expected. It is true that the *comprador*, or purveyor, with whom they contracted for provisions during their stay, went off with some of their money in his pockets; but that might have happened nearer home. And the old merchant, who had been engaged to use his interest in order to procure leave for Mr. King to proceed to Canton, shook himself almost to bits for sheer fright on finding out that that gentleman had gone thither without waiting for his passport; nay, that at the very time the worthy man was congratulating himself and his English friends on the success of his efforts, and the probable arrival of the document in a few days, the audacious officer was already in the city. But this piece of daring was quite enough to drive a "Celestial" distracted, and, his agitation, therefore, could not be wondered at.

At length, as nothing is denied to well-directed labour, all preparations were completed; but, before sailing, news reached our people, of war having broken out between the English and French, the United States taking sides with the latter. So they began to furbish up their artillery, and add stout bulwarks to the ships' sides, not knowing whether they might not have to fight their way home. To the honour of our enemies of that time, it was, however, discovered that both French and American vessels of war had received strict orders to respect and leave unmolested, if met with, the vessels that had sailed under Captain Cook's command. Their great guns were not, therefore, required, except for salutes; for Captain Gore could not do otherwise than follow so excellent an example, and refrain from any attempts at capture, tempting as might be the opportunities for it during his homeward course.

It was "up anchor" on the 12th January, 1780, and the two ships got out of Macao *Roads*—as the shallower waters that generally lie close to a coast are called. On the 20th, after some rough weather, fresh provisions and wood being required, they came to anchor again at a small crescent-shaped, mountainous island, where, by displaying a handful of dollars, their wish to buy buffaloes and fowls was quickly understood: and, with much snorting, ramping, and difficulty, a number of the former, some of the biggest of their kind, were got on board, where, strange to say, in the course of four-and-twenty hours, they became the tamest and mildest of all huge beasts. Two of them turned out quite sailors' pets; and Captain King was in hopes of bringing them to England, in order to introduce into this country so valuable a breed of cattle—for they had meat enough on their large bones to make them dear to graziers —but an unlucky accident disappointed him.

The refractoriness of these creatures, when it came to shipping them through the heavy surf, proved not to be regretted, for the time taken up by it gave opportunity for the finding of two wells of excellent water, a full supply of which, together with wood, put them into heart. Plenty of good fish had also been netted, and this, with the cabbage-palm, a very agreeable vegetable, the product of the country, had afforded them some welcome variety of diet. Fat pigs were also had, and the woods abounded with game; but the gentlemen who went out in pursuit of it were either bad shots, or the birds were even more unwilling to be bagged than birds generally are.

The inhabitants were natives of Cambodia and Cochin China, short, swarthy, and feeble-looking, who spoke the Malay language.

The sails of the two climate and storm-battered ships were furled "for good," as the phrase is, at the Nore, on the 2nd of October—all hands, save two or three, hale and well, after an absence from England of four years, two months, and twenty-two days.

"And so He bringeth them unto the haven where they would be."

THE END.

A SELECTION FROM

Cassell Petter & Galpin's Publications.

Picturesque Europe. Vols. I. to IV. now ready, each containing Thirteen exquisite Steel Plates from Original Drawings, and nearly 200 Original Illustrations on Wood. With Descriptive Letterpress. Royal 4to, cloth gilt, £2 2s. each ; morocco, £5 5s. each.
Vols. I. and II. contain GREAT BRITAIN *and* IRELAND *complete, £2 2s. each, or in One Vol., whole bound, extra gilt, gilt edges, £5 5s.*

The Magazine of Art. Volume I., containing about 200 Illustrations, including an Etching for Frontispiece by L. LOWENSTAM, from a Picture by FRANZ HALS. Extra crown 4to, cloth gilt, price 7s. 6d.

Pleasant Spots around Oxford. By ALFRED RIMMER. With numerous Original Illustrations. Extra fcap. 4to, cloth, gilt edges, 21s.

Familiar Wild Flowers. FIRST SERIES. By F. E. HULME, F.L.S., F.S.A., Art Master in Marlborough College. With Forty Full-page Coloured Plates, and Descriptive Text. Crown 8vo, cloth gilt, gilt edges, in cardboard box, 12s. 6d.

The Great Painters of Christendom, from Cimabue to Wilkie. By JOHN FORBES ROBERTSON. Illustrated throughout. Royal 4to, cloth elegant, gilt edges, £3 3s.

Royal Quarto Shakespeare. Edited by CHARLES and MARY COWDEN CLARKE, and containing about 600 Illustrations by H. C. SELOUS. Complete in Three Vols., cloth gilt, gilt edges, £3 3s.; morocco, £6 6s.

The Leopold Shakspere. Dedicated, by permission, to H.R.H. Prince Leopold. The Text of the Leopold Shakspere is that of Professor DELIUS, while an Introduction to the entire Work has been written by Mr. F. J. FURNIVALL. This Edition includes "The Two Noble Kinsmen," and "Edward III." With about 400 Illustrations. Small 4to, 1,184 pages, cloth, 10s. 6d.

The National Portrait Gallery. Complete in Four Volumes, each containing Twenty Portraits of our most distinguished Celebrities, printed in the highest style of Chromo-Lithography, with accompanying Memoirs, compiled from authentic sources. Cloth, 12s. 6d. each.

Old and New London. Complete in Six Volumes, each containing about 200 Illustrations. Extra crown 4to, cloth gilt, 9s. each.

The Races of Mankind. By ROBERT BROWN, M.A., F.R.G.S. With 500 Illustrations. Complete in Four Vols., extra crown 4to, cloth, 6s. each ; or in Two Vols., cloth, £1 1s.

The Countries of the World. By Dr. ROBERT BROWN, M.A., F.R.G.S., &c. Vols. I., II., and III., with about 140 Illustrations and Maps, extra crown 4to, cloth, 7s. 6d. each.

The Domestic Dictionary. Uniform with "Cassell's Dictionary of Cookery." An Encyclopædia for the Household. 1,280 pages, royal 8vo, half-roan, 15s.

Cookery, Cassell's Dictionary of. With numerous Engravings and full-page Coloured Plates. Containing about 9,000 Recipes. 1,180 pages, royal 8vo, cloth, 15s.

N.B.—For a List of the DORÉ FINE ART BOOKS, *see* **Cassell's Complete Catalogue,** *post free on application.*

Cassell Petter & Galpin : London, Paris & New York.

A Selection from Cassell Petter & Galpin's Publications (continued).

New Testament Commentary for English Readers. Edited by C. J. ELLICOTT, D.D., Lord Bishop of Gloucester and Bristol. Volume I. contains the Four Gospels, price 21s. Vol. II. contains The Acts, Romans, Corinthians, and Galatians, price 21s. Vol. III. contains the remaining Books of the New Testament, price 21s.

The Life of Christ. By the Rev. Canon FARRAR, D.D., F.R.S. *Illustrated Edition*, Complete in One Volume, extra crown 4to, cloth, gilt edges, price 21s.; calf or morocco, £2 2s. *Library Edition*, Complete in Two Volumes, Demy 8vo, cloth, 24s.; morocco, £2 2s.

The Half-Guinea Illustrated Bible. Containing 900 Original Illustrations specially executed for this Edition from Original Photographs and other authentic sources. Printed in clear readable type, with References. Crown 4to, strongly bound in cloth, 10s. 6d.

Russia. By D. MACKENZIE WALLACE, M.A. An Account of the Political, Social, and Domestic Life of the Russian People. *Cheap Edition*, One Vol., 10s. 6d. *Library Edition*, Two Vols., cloth, 24s.

The French Revolutionary Epoch. A History of France from the Beginning of the First Revolution to the End of the Second Empire. By HENRI VAN LAUN. Two Vols., demy 8vo, 24s.

The English Army: Its Past History, Present Condition, and Future Prospects. By Major ARTHUR GRIFFITHS, Author of "Memorials of Millbank," &c. Demy 8vo, cloth, 21s.

New Greece. By LEWIS SERGEANT. Demy 8vo, with Two Maps, Cloth, 21s.

A Ride to Khiva. By CAPTAIN BURNABY. With large Maps showing Districts Traversed, &c. *Cheap Edition*, cloth, 7s. 6d.

The Great Thirst Land. A Ride through Natal, Orange Free State, Transvaal, Kalahari. By PARKER GILLMORE ("Ubique"). *Cheap Edition*. Extra crown 8vo, cloth, 7s. 6d.

The Family Physician. A Manual of Domestic Medicine. By PHYSICIANS and SURGEONS of the Principal London Hospitals. Royal 8vo, price 21s.

England, Cassell's Illustrated History of, from the Earliest Period to the Present Time. With about 2,000 Illustrations. NEW TONED PAPER EDITION. Complete in Nine Vols., cloth, each, 9s. LIBRARY EDITION, bound in brown cloth, gilt tops, £4 10s.

Protestantism, The History of. By the Rev. J. A. WYLIE, LL.D. Complete in Three Vols., with upwards of 600 Original Illustrations. Cloth, £1 7s.

United States, Cassell's History of the. Complete in Three Vols., with 600 Illustrations, £1 7s.

Popular Educator, Cassell's New. Revised to the Present Date, with numerous Additions. Complete in Six Vols., 412 pages each, cloth, 6s. each; or Three Vols., half-calf, £2 10s.

Technical Educator, Cassell's. With Coloured Designs and numerous Illustrations. Complete in Four Vols., extra crown 4to, cloth, 6s. each; or Two Vols., half-calf, 31s. 6d.

Cassell Petter & Galpin: London, Paris & New York.

A Selection from Cassell Petter & Galpin's Publications (continued). 3

At the South Pole. By W. H. G. KINGSTON. With Forty Engravings. Crown 8vo, cloth, gilt edges, 5s.

Captain Cook, The Story of. By M. JONES. Illustrated with about Forty Engravings. Cloth, gilt edges, 5s.

Civil Service, Guide to Employment in the. With an Introduction by J. D. MORELL, LL.D. Cloth, 2s. 6d.

Common-sense Housekeeping. By PHILLIS BROWNE. With Illustrations. Extra fcap. 8vo, 250 pages, cloth, 2s. 6d.

Common-sense Cookery. By A. G. PAYNE. With Illustrations. 256 pages, extra fcap. 8vo, cloth, 2s. 6d.

Decisive Events in History. By THOMAS ARCHER. With 16 Original Illustrations. Extra fcap. 4to, 176 pages, cloth gilt, 5s.

Dictionary of Phrase and Fable; giving the Derivation, Source, or Origin of Common Phrases, Allusions, and Words that have a Tale to Tell. By the Rev. Dr. BREWER. Demy 8vo, 1,000 pages, cloth, 7s. 6d.

Dog, The. By IDSTONE. With Twelve Illustrations by G. EARL. Cloth, 2s. 6d.

Esther West. By ISA CRAIG-KNOX. Illustrated with Twenty-four Engravings. Imperial 16mo. Cloth, gilt edges, 5s.

Golden Days. By JEANIE HERING. The Experiences of an English Girl's School Life in Germany. Cloth, gilt edges, 5s.

Half-Hours with Early Explorers. By T. FROST. Profusely Illustrated. Cloth, 5s.

Historical Scenes. Containing some of the most striking Episodes from History. Selected by E. SPOONER. Cloth, 2s. 6d.

How to Get On. Edited by GODFREY GOLDING. With 1,000 Precepts for Practice. Cloth bevelled, gilt edges, 3s. 6d.

Magic Flower-Pot, The, and Other Stories. By EDWARD GARRETT, Author of "The Occupations of a Retired Life," "By Still Waters," &c. Crown 8vo, 292 pages, cloth gilt, 5s.

Manners of Modern Society. A Comprehensive Work on the Etiquette of the Present Day. Cloth gilt, 2s. 6d.

My Guardian. By ADA CAMBRIDGE. *Library Edition.* With Full-page Illustrations by FRANK DICKSEE, printed on Plate paper. Reprinted with Additions, from "Cassell's Family Magazine." Crown 8vo, cloth gilt, 6s.

Nestleton Magna. A Story of Yorkshire Methodism. By the Rev. J. JACKSON WRAY. Cloth, 3s. 6d.; cloth gilt, 5s.

North-West Passage by Land. By Viscount MILTON and Dr. CHEADLE. *Cheap Edition*, crown 8vo, cloth, 2s. 6d.; gilt edges, 3s. 6d.

Notable Shipwrecks. By UNCLE HARDY. Crown 8vo, 320 pages, with Frontispiece. Cloth gilt, 5s.

Nursing for the Home and for the Hospital, A Handbook of. By CATHERINE J. WOOD. Extra fcap. 8vo, cloth gilt, gilt edges, 3s. 6d.

Cassell Petter & Galpin: London, Paris & New York.

A Selection from Cassell Petter & Galpin's Publications (continued).

Palissy the Potter. By Professor HENRY MORLEY. *New Library Edition.* With Four Full-page Illustrations. Crown 8vo, 320 pages, cloth, 5s.

Peggy, and Other Tales. By FLORENCE MONTGOMERY. *New Library Edition, uniform with "Misunderstood."* Cloth lettered, 5s.

Peter Pengelly; or, True as the Clock. By the Rev. J. JACKSON WRAY. Crown 8vo, with Illustrations, cloth, 2s.

Pictures of School Life and Boyhood. Selected from the Best Authors, and Edited by PERCY FITZGERALD, M.A. Cloth, gilt edges, 3s. 6d.

Practical Kennel Guide, The. By Dr. GORDON STABLES. With Illustrations. Crown 8vo, 204 pages, cloth, 3s. 6d.

Practical Poultry-Keeper, The. By L. WRIGHT. With Illustrations. Cloth, 3s. 6d.; or Eight new Chromo Plates in addition, 5s.

Soldier and Patriot. The Story of GEORGE WASHINGTON. By F. M. OWEN. Cloth, bevelled boards, gilt edges, 256 pages, 3s. 6d.

Stories of Girlhood; or, The Brook and the River. A Book for Girls. By SARAH DOUDNEY. Illustrated. Extra fcap. 4to, cloth gilt, gilt edges, 5s.

Talks about Trees. A Popular Account of their Nature and Uses. By M. and E. KIRBY. Profusely Illustrated. Cloth, gilt edges, 3s. 6d.

The True Glory of Woman. By the Rev. DR. LANDELS. Crown 8vo, cloth, gilt edges, 3s. 6d.

The Three Homes. A Tale for Fathers and Sons. By F. T. L. HOPE. Crown 8vo, 400 pages, cloth, gilt edges, 5s.

The Theory and Action of the Steam Engine: for Practical Men. By W. H. NORTHCOTT, C.E. Demy 8vo, 224 pages, with numerous Diagrams and Tables, cloth, 7s. 6d.

Truth will Out. By JEANIE HERING, Author of "Golden Days," "Little Pickles," &c. Crown 8vo, 240 pages, cloth, gilt edges, 3s. 6d.

Wonders, Library of. A Series of Books for Boys. All profusely Illustrated, and bound in cloth gilt, gilt edges, 3s. 6d. each.

Wonders of Animal Instinct.
Wonders of Bodily Strength and Skill.
Wonders of Acoustics.
Wonders of Water.
Wonders of Architecture.
Wonderful Adventures.
Wonderful Balloon Ascents.
Wonderful Escapes.

Working to Win. By MAGGIE SYMINGTON. With Four full-page Illustrations. Cloth, gilt edges, 5s.

Young Man in the Battle of Life, The. By the Rev. Dr. LANDELS. Fcap. 8vo, 292 pages. Cloth gilt, 3s. 6d.

CASSELL'S COMPLETE CATALOGUE, *containing a Complete List of Works, including Bibles and Religious Literature, Children's Books, Dictionaries, Educational Works, Fine Art Volumes, Hand-books and Guides, History, Miscellaneous, Natural History, Poetry, Travels, Serials, sent post free on application to* CASSELL PETTER & GALPIN, Ludgate Hill, London.

www.ingramcontent.com/pod-product-compliance
Lightning Source LLC
Chambersburg PA
CBHW030254240426
43673CB00040B/965